C000304126

SYDNEY
ENCOUNTER

CHARLES RAWLINGS-WAY

Sydney Encounter
Published by Lonely Planet Publications Pty Ltd
ABN 36 005 607 983

Australia	Head Office, Locked Bag 1, Footscray, Vic 3011
	☎ 03 8379 8000 fax 03 8379 8111
	talk2us@lonelyplanet.com.au
USA	150 Linden St, Oakland, CA 94607
	☎ 510 893 8555
	toll free 800 275 8555
	fax 510 893 8572
	info@lonelyplanet.com
UK	72–82 Rosebery Avenue, Clerkenwell, London EC1R 4RW
	☎ 020 7841 9000 fax 020 7841 9001
	go@lonelyplanet.co.uk

This guidebook was commissioned in Lonely Planet's Melbourne office, and produced by the following: **Commissioning Editor** Meg Worby **Coordinating Editors** Monique Choy, Brooke Lyons **Coordinating Cartographers** Julie Sheridan, Anita Banh, Malisa Plesa **Coordinating Layout Designer** Jacqueline McLeod **Managing Editor** Geoff Howard **Managing Cartographers** David Connolly **Senior Editor** Katie Lynch **Assisting Layout Designers** Cara Smith, Katie Thuy Bui **Cover Designer** Wendy Wright **Project Manager** Rachel Imeson **Series Designer** Wendy Wright **Thanks to** Sally Darmody, Joshua Geoghegan, Emma Gilmour, Laura Jane, Trent Paton, Celia Wood

Our Readers Many thanks to the travellers who wrote to us with helpful hints, useful advice and interesting anecdotes: Coral Anderson, Maureen Ball, Richard Beatty, Nigel Chent, Sue Davidson, Elaine Evans, Richard Francis, Alexia Hollands, Anthony Keogh, Silke Kerwick, Rebecca Larratt, Julie Macklin, Norm & Mary Mainland, Alan Morrison, Peter Saundry, Ken Sutherland.

All images are copyright of the photographers unless otherwise indicated. Many of the images in this guide are available for licensing from **Lonely Planet Images**: www.lonelyplanetimages.com.

ISBN 987 1 74059 839 2

Printed through Colorcraft Ltd, Hong Kong.
Printed in China.

Acknowledgements Sydney Ferries Corporation Network Map © 2007 Sydney Ferries Corporation; CityRail Sydney Suburban Network Map © 2006 RailCorp

HOW TO USE THIS BOOK
Colour-Coding & Maps

Colour-coding is used for symbols on maps and in the text that they relate to (eg all eating venues on the maps and in the text are given a green fork symbol). Each neighbourhood also gets its own colour, and this is used down the edge of the page and throughout that neighbourhood section.

Shaded yellow areas on the maps denote 'areas of interest' – for their historical significance, their attractive architecture or their great bars and restaurants. We encourage you to head to these areas and just start exploring!

Prices

Multiple prices listed with reviews (eg $10/5 or $10/5/20) indicate adult/child, adult/concession or adult/child/family.

Send us your feedback We love to hear from readers – your comments help make our books better. We read every word you send us, and we always guarantee that your feedback goes straight to the appropriate authors. The most useful submissions are rewarded with a free book. To send us your updates and find out about Lonely Planet events, newsletters and travel news visit our award-winning website: *lonelyplanet .com/contact*

Note: We may edit, reproduce and incorporate your comments in Lonely Planet products such as guidebooks, websites and digital products, so let us know if you don't want your comments reproduced or your name acknowledged. For a copy of our privacy policy visit *lonelyplanet.com/privacy*

CHARLES RAWLINGS-WAY

Born in Devonshire and transported to Tasmania when he was three, Charles lusted after Sydney for far too long before mustering the nerve to ask for a date. And to his amazement, she said yes! The city's cool bars and warm beaches proved predictably seductive – lust soon turned into love and an inescapable fascination.

A lapsed architect, underrated rock guitarist, optimistic home renovator and confirmed hedonist, Charles greased the production cogs at Lonely Planet's Melbourne HQ for many moons before hitting the open road as a freelance travel writer a few years ago. He regularly flees Melbourne's calmer cultures for a walk on Sydney's wild side, and to visit his mum.

CHARLES' THANKS

Thanks to the following folks for their input, generosity, friendship and distraction during the creation of this book: Megan Worby, Mona and Olivia Rawlings-Way, Warren and Nathan Jones, Julie Sheridan, Jay Chinchen, Lauren Walter, Jenny Blake, Rodney and Sandra Renshaw, Rod and Cathy Connelly, Catherine Mundy, Carl Panczak and the LP production crew.

Above all, thank you Meg for our truly inescapable fascination.

THE PHOTOGRAPHER

With a burning desire to document the unusual, Travis Drever has spent a good part of the last two decades snapping happily at anything that takes his fancy. Shooting for a varied range of corporates including *The Herald and Weekly Times* and *mX* as well as donating his services to *MiniBar Magazine* and *The Green Left Weekly*, he now has a Lonely Planet commission under his belt. Australian-born, Travis has had to clock up many a frequent flyer-point in his plight to find that perfect image: he has travelled throughout Asia and lived in Spain, Sweden, Holland, England and France.

Cover photograph Bondi Icebergs at dawn, Charlotte Fenton/Alamy. **Internal photographs** p82, p93, p130 by Charles Rawlings-Way; p20 courtesy the City of Sydney; p101, 135, 137/Peter Dragicevich; p21 courtesy Tropfest; p159 Ben Symons/courtesy the artist and Annandale Galleries, Sydney. All other photographs by Lonely Planet Images, and by Travis Drever except p4, p6 Oliver Strewe; p12 Claver Carroll; p19 John Borthwick; p22, p40 Paul Beinssen; p34 Glenn Beanland; p46, p70, p115, p149, p151 Greg Elms.

Sunny side up: the Sculpture by the Sea (p22) exhibition

CONTENTS

THIS IS SYDNEY

At the heart of Sydney – Australia's oldest, largest and most diverse city – is the outrageously good-looking Sydney Harbour. Like a psychedelic supermodel, the city curves and sways through a glamorous maze of sandstone headlands, lazy bays and legendary surf beaches.

The Sydney experience is essentially physical: dunk yourself in the Bondi surf, sail under the Harbour Bridge on a yacht, jog along the Bondi clifftops or just yell yourself hoarse at a rugby match. Outside is where you want to be – the beaches swarm, street cafés buzz and the harbour blooms with sails.

No less culturally complex than it is on the map, Sydney is the landing point for most of Australia's immigrants. An edgy multiculturalism ignites the city's food scene and fuels its nocturnal life – you'll lose yourself in the restaurants, bars and dance clubs just as easily as on the streets. Aboriginal heritage makes an impact through art – a crop of excellent urban galleries celebrating indigenous culture.

Jealous as hell, the rest of Australia stereotypes Sydney as more body-beautiful than bookish, more carpe diem than museum – a narcissistic 'Sin City' fixated on sunglasses, salons and soy lattes. Sure, there's a lot of blonde dye in Bondi, but Sydney's citizens are no prettier than anyone else. The genetic legacy of the British and Irish convicts who built the city is more evident in the city's dogged self-belief than anything mirror-worthy. Make no mistake – Sydneysiders invest heavily in aesthetics, but their infectious, gutsy energy overrides the glam and relegates big-city cynicism, suburban sprawl and occasional racial friction to the back of their collective mind.

From squalid and desperate penal beginnings, it's no small irony that Sydney has evolved into a sparkling, progressive metropolis defined by optimism and staggering natural beauty. The rest of Australia is in denial – Sydney is as good as it gets!

Top Left Opera Bar (p59) **Top Right** Boathouse on Blackwattle Bay (p81) **Bottom** Bronte Beach (p14)

>HIGHLIGHTS

Browse for classy souvenirs in the Opera House Shop

HIGHLIGHTS

>1 SYDNEY OPERA HOUSE

SWOON BENEATH THE HEAVEN-SENT CURVES OF THE SYDNEY OPERA HOUSE

Aghast with admiration for the Sydney Opera House, famous architect Louis Kahn said: 'The sun did not know how beautiful its light was until it was reflected off this building.' Danish architect Jørn Utzon's competition-winning 1956 design is Australia's most recognisable icon. Utzon is rumoured to have drawn inspiration from orange segments, palm fronds and Mayan temples, and the building has been poetically likened to a typewriter stuffed with scallop shells and the sexual congress of turtles. Viewed from any angle it's architecturally orgasmic, but the ferry view approaching Circular Quay is hard to beat.

The predicted four-year construction started in 1959. After a tumultuous tirade of ego clashes, delays, politicking, death and cost blowouts, Utzon quit in disgust in 1966. The Opera House finally opened in 1973. Unembittered, Utzon and his son Jan were commissioned for renovations in 2004.

Inside are four main auditoriums where dance, concerts, opera and theatre are staged (p62), plus the left-of-centre studio for emerging artists. The acoustics are superb; the internal aesthetics like the belly of a whale. Most events (2400 of them annually!) sell out quickly, but partial-view tickets are often available on short notice. There's also an exhibition hall and an artsy Sunday market on the concourse (p54).

See also p53.

>2 SYDNEY HARBOUR BRIDGE

TRAVEL ACROSS, OVER OR UNDER THE SYDNEY HARBOUR BRIDGE

Whether they're driving over it, climbing up it, rollerblading across it or sailing under it, Sydneysiders adore their bridge and swarm around it like ants on ice cream. Dubbed the 'old coat hanger', it's a spookily big object – moving around town you'll catch sight of it out of the corner of your eye and get a fright! Perhaps Sydney poet Kenneth Slessor said it best: 'Day and night, the bridge trembles and echoes like a living thing.'

The bridge links the CBD with North Sydney, crossing the harbour at one of its narrowest points. The two halves of chief engineer JJC Bradfield's mighty arch – 134m high and 502m long – were built outwards from each shore. In 1932, after nine years of merciless toil, the two arches were only centimetres apart when 100km/h winds set them swaying. The coat hanger hung tough and the arch was soon completed. In 2007 the bridge turned 75.

The best way to experience the bridge is on foot – don't expect much of a view crossing by car or train. Staircases access the bridge from both shores; a footpath runs along its eastern side. If this view doesn't sate you, try a knee-trembling BridgeClimb (p60) or scale the southeast pylon to the Pylon Lookout Museum.

See also p52.

>3 SYDNEY HARBOUR

SAIL OUT ONTO SYDNEY HARBOUR, THE WET ESSENCE OF SYDNEY

When convicted murderer Francis Morgan stood on the Pinchgut Island gallows in 1797, about to hang, he gazed wistfully across Sydney Harbour and uttered, 'Well, you have here indeed a most beautiful harbour.' Morgan had a point. Stretching 20km inland, the harbour is the shimmering soul of Sydney, its beaches, coves, bays, islands and waterside parks providing crucial relief from the ordeals of urban life. Crisscrossed by ferries and carpeted by yachts, it's both the city's playground and a major port.

The chardonnay way to experience Sydney Harbour is to go sailing (p75). Alternatively, catch the ferry to Manly (p132), swim at Shark Bay (p15), dine with harbour views at Circular Quay (p55), or chase the harbour upstream to Parramatta (p27) on a RiverCat (p175).

Sydney Harbour National Park protects pockets of harbourside bushland (with some magical walking tracks including the Manly Scenic Walkway, p142), and five harbour islands. Clark, Shark and Rodd islands are chilled-out picnic spots – the Sydney Visitor Centre (p180) provides access info. Goat Island and Fort Denison (aka 'Pinchgut') were once hellish convict gulags. Goat Island is off-limits, but the National Parks & Wildlife Service (p180) runs Fort Denison tours.

North Head and South Head form the gateway to the harbour. Our South Head Shuffle walking tour (p143) takes in Watsons Bay and the Gap, an epic clifftop lookout.

>4 KINGS CROSS & AROUND

SLICE THROUGH THE VICE AROUND KINGS CROSS, SYDNEY'S EDGIEST ENCLAVE

Riding high above the CBD beneath the big Coca-Cola sign (as much a Sydney icon as LA's Hollywood sign), 'the Cross' is a bizarre, densely populated dichotomy of good and evil. Strip joints, tacky tourist shops and backpacker hostels bang heads with classy restaurants, funky bars and gorgeous guesthouses as the Cross pumps 24/7. A weird cross-section of society is drawn to the lights – buskers, beggars, tourists, prostitutes, pimps, groomed metrosexuals, horny businessmen and underfed artists roam the streets on equal footing. The Cross rocks.

Smitten with a hooker in his ode 'Darling It Hurts', brilliant Aussie songwriter Paul Kelly sang, 'Darling it hurts to see you down in Darlinghurst tonight'. Kings Cross prostitutes rarely venture across William St into Darlinghurst these days – there are too many cinematographers and caffeinated students wanting to smell the action without necessarily getting involved.

Woolloomooloo, down McElhone Stairs from the Cross, has also cleaned up its act. Harry's Café de Wheels (p102) and the sailors remain, but things are begrudgingly less pugilistic than in the past.

Gracious, tree-lined Potts Point and Elizabeth Bay seem worlds away. Well-preserved Victorian, Edwardian and Art Deco houses and flats flank picturesque avenues. Elizabeth Bay House (p97) is a must-see.

See also p96.

> 5 BEACHES, BEACHES, BEACHES

CARVE UP THE SURF OR SUN YOURSELF SILLY ON SYDNEY'S FABULOUS BEACHES

Sydney's beaches – protected harbour enclaves and surf-pummelled ocean shores – teem with weekend life, but Sydneysiders also swim before, after or instead of going to work. Most beaches are clean, accessible and patrolled by surf lifesavers. Many beaches are topless; a couple are nude (when in Rome…).

Definitively Sydney, Bondi is one of the world's great beaches – the Pacific arrives in great foaming swells and all people are equal, as democratic as sand. It's the closest ocean beach to the city, has good waves and is great for a rough 'n' tumble swim. Don't miss the Bondi Pavilion (p123), Sunday's Bondi Markets (p123), the Bondi to Bronte Clifftop Trail (p140) and the Eora Aboriginal rock engravings near the cliffs at the Bondi Beach Golf Club, north of the beach.

South of Bondi are Tamarama, Bronte, Coogee, Maroubra and Cronulla beaches. Fully deserving of the nickname 'Glamarama', Tamarama's deep, sexy gulch attracts the generically gorgeous. Bronte is a small family-oriented beach with a perfect rock pool and a string of beachy cafés. Coogee is an Aboriginal word for rotting seaweed, but don't let that deter you – the beach is wide and handsome. Maroubra rivals Bondi for size and swell, but it's far more relaxed. Cronulla's *looong* surf beach stretches towards Botany Bay's refineries. It's an

edgy place, the ragged sense of impending 'something' erupting into racial violence in late 2005.

Worthy harbour beaches include Camp Cove, Shark Bay and Balmoral. Camp Cove is a gorgeous golden beach frequented by Watsons Bay families and topless beach babes. Despite the name, there's really nothing to worry about at Shark Bay – a hefty net protects swimmers from becoming something's lunch. Balmoral is popular with picnicking North Shore families, swimmers, kayakers and windsurfers.

Beyond Manly, King of the Northern Beaches, are dozens of beaut beaches. Capped by Barrenjoey Lighthouse, Palm Beach is a meniscus of bliss. Nudists nude-up to the north, million-dollar real estate booms in the south and cheesy TV soap *Home & Away* is filmed somewhere in between. Sleepy Whale Beach is underrated – a paradisaical slice of deep, orange sand flanked by steep cliffs. Caught in a sandy '70s time-warp, Avalon is the mythical Australian beach you always dreamed was there but could never find. When the *Baywatch* producers wanted to film here in the '90s, locals told them to bugger off!

Elongated Narrabeen, immortalised by the Beach Boys in *Surfin' USA*, chases the endless summer south to Collaroy – high-rise apartments and high-rise surf dominate. Distorted from *diwai*, an Aboriginal name for a local bird, Dee Why is a no-fuss family beach with chunky apartments, cafés and *Big Wednesday* breaks.

See p122 for more on Bondi, Bronte and Coogee and p132 for more on Manly.

>6 THE ROCKS

SIFT THROUGH THE BONES OF HISTORY IN THE ROCKS

Sydney's first European settlement at The Rocks was a squalid, over-crowded place. Residents sloshed through open sewers; alleyways festered with disease, prostitution and drunken lawlessness.

Shipping services relocated in the 1800s, bubonic plague broke out in 1900, and Harbour Bridge construction in the '20s razed entire streets. It wasn't until the 1970s that The Rocks' cultural and architectural heritage was finally recognised. Redevelopment saved many old buildings, but the area has become an 'olde-worlde' tourist trap. Shops hocking Opera House key-rings proliferate, but gritty history is never far below the surface if you know where to look. Check out Cadman's Cottage (p50), Susannah Place (p52) and the Rocks Discovery Museum (p51). The weekend Rocks Market (p55) is a good excuse to sniff around.

Next door is Millers Point, a low-key colonial district. Garrison Church (1848, Australia's oldest) faces Argyle Place, an English-style village green on which every Australian has the legal right to graze livestock. Nearby, the Lord Nelson Brewery Hotel (p59) and Hero of Waterloo on Windmill St jostle for supreme respect as Australia's oldest pub. Here you'll also find the Sydney Observatory (p52) and the SH Ervin Gallery (p51).

At Walsh Bay you'll find the Sydney Theatre Company (p63), Bangarra Dance Theatre (p59), Sydney Dance Company (p61) and Sydney Theatre (p62).

See also p48.

>7 ROYAL BOTANIC GARDENS

GRAZE THE AFTERNOON AWAY IN THE ROYAL BOTANIC GARDENS

The Royal Botanic Gardens (RBG) were established in 1816 as the colony's veggie patch. The attitude here is relaxed – signs say, 'Please walk on the grass. We also invite you to smell the roses, hug the trees, talk to the birds and picnic on the lawns'. Go exploring, take a free guided walk, or jump on the trackless train if you've outdone yourself.

Highlights include the rose garden, the South Pacific plant collection, the prickly arid garden, the Tropical Centre's glass pyramid and a sinister bat colony (a murder of bats?). Management periodically tries to oust the bats as they destroy the vegetation, but they just keep hanging around…

The gardens' northeastern tip is Mrs Macquaries Point, a functional lookout long before Europeans arrived. It was named in 1810 after Elizabeth, Governor Macquarie's wife, who ordered a chair chiselled into the rock from which she'd view the harbour.

Government House (p50) governs the gardens' northwest sector. The Domain is a large grassy tract linking the RBG and Hyde Park, preserved by Governor Phillip in 1788 for public recreation. The lawns host free summer concerts, Sunday's eccentric Speakers' Corner (p36), and Carols by Candlelight every Christmas. The Art Gallery of NSW (p18) is here, too.

See also p35.

HIGHLIGHTS

>8 ART GALLERY OF NSW

HANG WITH THE MASTERS AT THE ART GALLERY OF NSW

Playing a prominent and gregarious role in Sydney society is the ultra-reputable Art Gallery of NSW. The gallery was established in 1874, when five trustees were appointed to administer a £500 grant from the NSW government towards 'the formation of a gallery of art'. Initially procuring paintings by Sydney and London artists, their vision expanded towards establishing an indigenous collection in the '60s.

Architecturally challenging extensions in the '70s, '90s and 2003 swelled the gallery's ambition further. Today, blockbuster international touring exhibitions arrive regularly (Man Ray, Caravaggio etc), and the gallery houses the world's most broadly representative collection of Australian art.

There are three permanent collections – the European, Australian and Asian Galleries. The controversial Archibald Prize for Australian portraiture exhibits here annually, as do the Wynne Prize (landscape or figure sculpture) and Sulman Prize (subject or mural painting) exhibitions, and the Artexpress exhibition of the year's best Higher School Certificate student art. Kids swarm to the GalleryKids Sunday programme, offering workshops, performances and free guided tours with costumed actors. There are also concerts, screenings, courses, celebrity talks and programs for the deaf and visually impaired. Speakers' Corner (p36) happens on Sunday afternoons on the lawns out front.

See also p34.

>SYDNEY DIARY

Festivals and events pepper Sydney's social calendar like... well, like pepper. Concert halls and theatres pack 'em in, but it's difficult to keep Sydneysiders inside for long. Sure, locals have season subscriptions to the Sydney Symphony and Sydney Theatre Company, but with so many sunny shores, earnest indoor pursuits often take a back seat.

Sydney's streets are crammed with 60,000 sweaty bodies during the annual City2Surf (p21) fun run.

JANUARY

Sydney Festival

www.sydneyfestival.org.au

Throughout January, Sydney's premiere arts and culture festival revolves around a central theme, expressed through musical, stage and street performance, visual art and 'happenings' around town. International and Australian performers run the gamut from opera to surreal gymnastics and water puppetry. Free shows aplenty.

Big Day Out

www.bigdayout.com

International music mosh at Sydney Olympic Park. Much head-banging, sun and beer.

Chinese New Year

www.cityofsydney.nsw.gov.au/cny

January/February — food, fireworks, dance, acrobatics, buskers, Chinatown parade and Darling Harbour dragon-boat races.

Flickerfest

www.flickerfest.com.au

International short film festival at Bondi Pavilion (p123) — shorts, documentaries, animation and workshops. Tours nationally.

FEBRUARY

Gay & Lesbian Mardi Gras

www.mardigras.org.au

A month-long festival and fleshy Oxford St parade. Gyms empty out, solariums

Gawk at the frocked-up and fabulous at Sydney's Gay & Lesbian Mardi Gras

darken, waxing emporiums tally profits. And 700,000 people like to watch; after-party tickets are gold.

Tropfest

www.tropfest.com.au

The world's largest short-film festival. Films incorporate a surprise 'signature' prop (kiss, bubble, sneeze etc). Free screenings; celeb judges (David Wenham, Gabriel Byrne, Salma Hayek).

....

MAY

Australian Fashion Week

www.afw.com.au

Long-legged waifs (of both sexes) strut and pout around Circular Quay. Expect high-profile designers from Australia and the Asia-Pacific region.

Sydney Writers Festival

www.swf.org.au

Readings with social, literary and political writers from Australia and overseas. Not afraid of the big issues; fresh talent abounds.

....

JUNE

Sydney Biennale

www.biennaleofsydney.com.au

In even-numbered years; international contemporary arts at the Art Gallery of NSW (p18) and city venues.

Go troppo at Tropfest

Darling Harbour International Jazz Festival

www.darlingharbour.com

Free jazzy jamboree. Eclectic artists such as James Morrison, Frank Bennett and the Cat Empire.

Sydney Film Festival

www.sydneyfilmfestival.org

Long-running film fiesta celebrating the human condition; global and local releases.

....

AUGUST

City2Surf

www.city2surf.sunherald.com.au

On the second Sunday in August, 60,000 highly trained athletes, overfed pretenders

SYDNEY DIARY

and sundry fools run (or walk) 14km from Hyde Park to Bondi Beach. The fastest reach the beach in 40 minutes, their athletic seriousness counterbalanced by family fun and the odd cardiac scare.

SEPTEMBER

Royal Botanic Gardens Spring Festival

www.rbgsyd.nsw.gov.au
Concerts, brass bands, plant markets and flower displays in early or mid-September.

Festival of the Winds

www.waverley.nsw.gov.au/info
/pavilion/fotw
The second Sunday in September; a multi-cultural kite-flying fiesta at Bondi Beach.

National Rugby League Grand Final

www.nrl.com.au
The big men collide in the NRL season finale; Aussie Stadium or Telstra Stadium.

NOVEMBER

Sculpture by the Sea

www.sculpturebythesea.com
In mid-November, the clifftop trail from Bondi Beach to Tamarama transforms into an exquisite sculpture garden. Serious prize money is on offer for the most creative, curious or quizzical offerings from

Head's up! Sculpture by the Sea

international and local sculptors. Bondi chefs cook up gourmet barbecue edibles for sculpture fans.

DECEMBER

Sydney to Hobart Yacht Race

www.rolexsydneyhobart.com
On 26 December Sydney Harbour churns with competitors and onlookers for the start of the world's most arduous open-ocean yacht race.

New Year's Eve

www.cityofsydney.nsw.gov.au/nye
Find someone with a penthouse or a yacht to watch the annual fireworks displays over Sydney Harbour. The bridge erupts with pyrotechnic bedazzlement.

Hang out at the Royal Botanic Gardens (p17)

ITINERARIES

If you've only got a day or three to make Sydney's acquaintance, try the following itineraries. Most of Sydney's signature attractions make the grade here, along with some rewarding local hangouts. Alternatively, beat a retreat from the crowds, escape the city on a day trip, or hunt down some free entertainment.

DAY ONE

Ramble down through The Rocks (p16) to Sydney Cove, then out past the Sydney Opera House (p10) to the Royal Botanic Gardens (p17). Grab a cab to Bondi Beach (p122) and dunk yourself in the Pacific. Suitably salted, swill a pre-dinner drink at the Opera Bar (p59), then catch an evening show at the Sydney Opera House (p62). Afterwards, some fresh seafood, divine Australian wine and harbour hubbub at a Circular Quay restaurant (p55) is hard to beat.

DAY TWO

Kick-start your day/heart with a BridgeClimb (p60) over the Sydney Harbour Bridge. Hang with the masters at the Art Gallery of NSW (p34) or ship yourself out onto the harbour: ride the ferry to Taronga Zoo (p134), or to Manly (p132) for a surf or a few hours of beachy empty-headedness. Chug a cold beer at Manly Wharf Hotel (p136), chow-down in Chinatown (p71) then hit some Darlinghurst bars (p104) for a jazzy nightcap.

DAY THREE

Sleep late, caffeinate at Campos (p81), then splash some cash in Paddington's Oxford St boutiques (p113). In the afternoon, make some fishy friends at the Sydney Aquarium (p68) or soar up Sydney Tower (p36) for eye-popping 360-degree views. Head to Darling Harbour for dinner (p71), cool your boots in Cargo Bar (p73), then heat your heels at one of Sydney's hellishly good clubs.

Top left Sharpen your haggling skills at Paddington Market (p116) **Top right** The Opera Bar (p59) provides dinner with a view **Bottom** Surfin' Bondi (p131) is the quintessential Sydney experience

ITINERARIES

FORWARD PLANNING

Three weeks before you go Check out some of the key Sydney websites (p177); get to know what's going on – both in the headlines and after hours – online by reading the local media (p178); check to see if your visit coincides with any major holidays or festivals (p19); make sure your passport and other documents are in order.

One week before you go Book tickets for any major concerts or shows that might interest you at places like the Sydney Opera House (p62) or the Sydney Theatre Company (p63); book a table at Aria (p55) or Tetsuya's (p43); remind your mother that she promised to feed the cat during your absence.

The day before you go Reconfirm your flight; check the Sydney websites for any last-minute changes or cancellations at entertainment venues; buy some Australian dollars; cancel the milk.

OFF THE BEATEN TRACK

Beat the heat at Balmoral Beach (p15) on the north shore with some top-notch restaurants and super swimming. At the end of Glebe Point Rd is Jubilee Park (Map p77, B2): snooze in the sun, throw a Frisbee or consume your airport novel under a gargantuan Moreton Bay fig. South of Coogee, oversized Maroubra Beach (p15) has underrated waves and a suburban tempo. West of the madding Rocks is Millers Point (Map p49, B3) where you'll find photogenic terraces, unpretentious pubs and picnic perfection at Sydney Observatory Park (Map p49, B3). Not far from Kings Cross, Rushcutters Bay Park offers uncrowded lawns where the pontoons bump and sway.

FREE STUFF

The Art Galley of NSW is artfully free, while free summer entertainment proliferates with regular musical performances in Sydney's parks. January's Sydney Festival (p20) offers dozens of outdoor events; October's **Manly International Jazz Festival** (www.manly.nsw.gov.au/manlyjazz/) and June's Darling Harbour International Jazz Festival (p21) have free outdoor gigs too. The Tropfest (p21) short-film festival in February has free screenings in The Domain and Darlinghurst.

Catch some street theatre and a few buskers at Sydney's weekend markets (p157), or around Circular Quay (p48), Martin Place (p32) or Darling Harbour (p64). The mad, the erudite and the madly erudite vent spleen at Speakers' Corner (p36) on Sunday afternoons. When all else fails, you can't beat a beach and a book (p15).

DAY TRIPPER

Free day up your sleeve? The Sydney Visitor Centre (p180) provides day-trip information.

The **Blue Mountains** (www.australiabluemountains.com.au), 110km west of Sydney, offer jaw-dropping scenery, bushwalks, gorges, gums and gourmet restaurants galore.

Tracking 30km north from Manly (p132), Sydney's sublime **Northern Beaches** (www.sydneynorthernbeaches.com.au) feature laid-back 'burbs, gnarly breaks, craggy headlands and fish-and-chip shops.

Ku-ring-gai Chase National Park (www.nationalparks.nsw.gov.au), 24km north of Sydney, has that classic Sydney cocktail of bushland, sandstone and water.

Royal National Park (www.nationalparks.nsw.gov.au), 30km south of the city, features vertiginous cliffs, secluded beaches, coastal scrub, seaside communities and cockatoos.

Parramatta (www.parracity.nsw.gov.au), 24km west of Sydney, was Australia's second European settlement. The town has been subsumed by suburbia, but retains a small-town vibe and a clutch of colonial buildings.

>NEIGHBOURHOODS

Beautiful Bronte (p122) proves it really is all that

NEIGHBOURHOODS

Central Sydney grips Sydney Harbour (aka Port Jackson) in a passionate embrace. The harbour runs east–west, dividing the city in two – the Sydney Harbour Bridge and Harbour Tunnel connect the south and north shores. The city centre and most of the action is south of the harbour.

Downtown Sydney's flooded with bistros, shops and cool bars that go bump in the night, but the city centre is largely abandoned to the skateboarders on weekends. North of the centre, The Rocks and Circular Quay are tourist meccas with superb restaurants, the Sydney Opera House sitting just northeast of Circular Quay. Southwest of the centre is Chinatown where paper dragons and fireworks temper the shameless restaurant spruikers on Dixon St. Northwest of here is Darling Harbour, an architecturally psychotic tourist haven where boardwalks, museums, restaurants, bars, hotel monoliths and freeway flyovers distract the masses.

The Inner West begins just west of Darling Harbour. Cafés and bookshops tangle with dreadlocked bohemia in Glebe, while grungy Newtown is King of the Inner West – tattoos, tofu and students rule on King St.

South of the city centre, Surry Hills brims with great places to eat and drink and bears absolutely no resemblance to Surry, England. In Darlinghurst, east of the centre, cafés bulge with cinematographers, thespians and gym-junkies buffing up for Mardi Gras. Infamous Kings Cross stews in its own sleazy, strangely hypnotic brand of sex, drugs and rock 'n' roll. South and west of here, Paddington and Woollahra set Sydney's social high-water mark with avant-garde galleries, gorgeous terrace houses and fabulous boutiques, while everything's pretty in pink along Oxford St, Sydney's gay hub.

Sydney's quintessential ocean suburb is Bondi (surfboards, sushi, internet, beer – take your pick). The eastern beaches track south from Bondi, including family-friendly Bronte and backpacker Coogee.

Across the bridge from The Rocks is the North Shore, the jewel of which is Manly, a beachy, affable 'burb where the surf's as good as the kebabs.

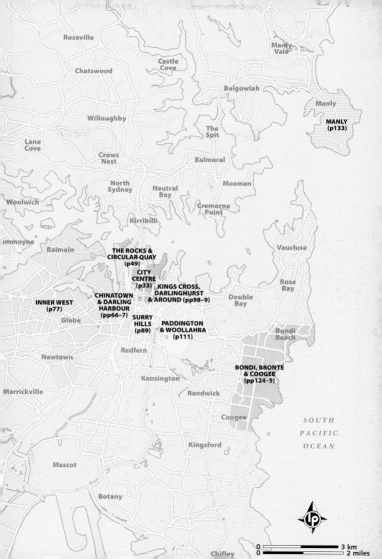

Roseville

Chatswood

Castle
Cove

Manly
Vale

Balgowlah

Manly

MANLY
(p133)

Willoughby

The Spit

Lane
Cove

Crows
Nest

Balmoral

Woolwich

North
Sydney

Neutral
Bay

Mosman

Immoyne

Kirribilli

Cremorne
Point

Balmain

Vaucluse

THE ROCKS &
CIRCULAR QUAY
(p49)

CITY
CENTRE
(p33)

Rose
Bay

INNER WEST
(p77)

CHINATOWN
& DARLING
HARBOUR
(pp66–7)

KINGS CROSS,
DARLINGHURST
& AROUND (pp98–9)

Double
Bay

Glebe

SURRY
HILLS
(p89)

PADDINGTON
& WOOLLAHRA
(p111)

Bondi
Beach

Newtown

Redfern

BONDI, BRONTE
& COOGEE
(pp124–5)

Marrickville

Kensington

Randwick

Coogee

SOUTH

PACIFIC

OCEAN

Kingsford

Mascot

Botany

0 ——————— 3 km
0 ——————— 2 miles

Chifley

>CITY CENTRE

Sydney's city centre erupts as lunchtime business bods splash cash in the shops and department stores around Pitt St Mall and Martin Place, and the classy shopping centres along George St. In between purchases they power-lunch at some of the city's most prestigious restaurants. There's a slew of hip, after-work bars here too, many of which slide seamlessly into jazzy, clubby moods later in the night. Clinging to the CBD fringes are some stellar museums, gracious colonial buildings and leafy retreats. The strip of greenery from Hyde Park, undulating through The Domain down to the Royal Botanic Gardens provides a vital counterpoint to the clash and throb of Sydney's commerce; office workers roll up their sleeves, munch falafels and slip off their shoes in the sun. Don't expect much downtown action on weekends though – on Sunday afternoons a sense of desolation weighs down, punctuated only by the occasional tumbleweed rolling through.

CITY CENTRE

◉ SEE

Art Gallery of NSW	1	D3
Australian Museum	2	C5
Hyde Park Barracks Museum	3	C3
Museum of Sydney	4	B1
Parliament House	5	C3
Royal Botanic Gardens	6	D2
Speakers' Corner	7	D3
St James' Church	8	B3
Sydney Tower & Skywalk	9	B4
Watters Gallery	10	D5

🛍 SHOP

David Jones	11	B4
David Jones	12	B4
Fairfax & Roberts	13	B3
Hobbyco	14	A4
Kinokuniya	15	A5
Love & Hatred	(see 24)	
Marcs	16	B3
Martin & Stein	(see 20)	

Myer	17	A4
Oroton	18	B3
Paspaley Pearls	19	B3
Queen Victoria Building	20	A4
Red Eye Records	21	A3
Red Eye Records	22	B6
RM Williams	23	A3
Strand Arcade	24	A3
Strand Hatters	(see 24)	
Tiffany & Co	25	C2
World Square	26	A6

🍴 EAT

Bar Reggio	27	D6
Bécasse	28	A4
Bodhi	29	C4
Est	30	A2
Forty One	31	B2
Mother Chu's Vegetarian Kitchen	32	A6
Prime	33	A3
Tetsuya's	34	A5

🍸 DRINK

Arthouse	35	B4
Bar Europa	36	B3
Bavarian Bier Café	37	A3
Establishment	(see 30)	
Hemmesphere	(see 30)	
Orbit Bar	38	A2
Redoak	39	A3
Tank Stream Bar	40	B2
Zeta	41	A4

⭐ PLAY

City Recital Hall	42	A3
Conservatorium of Music	43	C1
Metro	44	A6
Sydney Architecture Walks	(see 4)	
Tank	(see 40)	
Wine Banq	45	B3

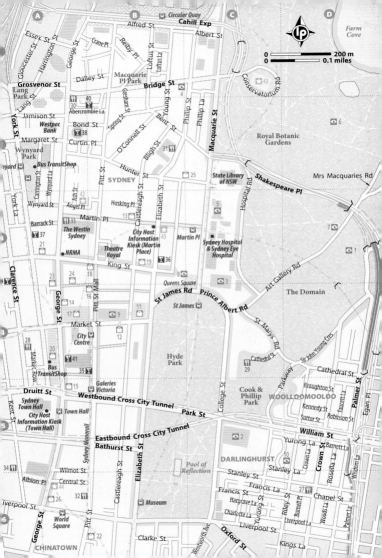

SEE

ART GALLERY OF NSW

☎ 9225 1744; www.artgallery.nsw
.gov.au; Art Gallery Rd, The Domain;
admission free, special exhibits vary;
🕙 10am-5pm Thu-Tue, to 9pm Wed;
🚊 St James 🚌 441; ♿

Don't miss classic Australian
paintings by Brett Whiteley, Arthur
Streeton, Sidney Nolan and Lloyd
Reese, and the Yiribana Gallery's
Aboriginal and Torres Strait Islander
art. The Sunday GalleryKids activity
programme includes dance, stories,
magic, cartoons and Aboriginal performance. Tours of the Asian Gallery
with Zhenmu Shou, a ghostly guide
from the grave, are a blast from the
past. See also p18.

Dream in colour at the Museum of Sydney

☉ AUSTRALIAN MUSEUM

☎ 9320 6000; www.amonline.net.au; 6-8 College St; admission $10/5, special exhibits extra; ☼ 9.30am-5pm; ⓜ Museum ⓜ Galeries Victoria; ♿

Established just 40 years after the First Fleet dropped anchor, this natural history museum features excellent native wildlife and Aboriginal exhibitions. There are self-guided tours, indigenous performances on Sundays and opportunities for kids to get busy in the Skeleton and Search & Discover galleries.

☉ HYDE PARK BARRACKS MUSEUM

☎ 8239 2311; www.hht.net.au; Queens Sq; admission $10/5, introductory room free; ☼ 9.30am-5pm; ⓜ St James ⓜ City Centre

Designed by prolific convict architect Francis Greenway, the barracks were used as convict quarters for Anglo-Irish sinners (1819–48), an immigrant depot (1848–86) and government courts (1887–1979) before their current incarnation – a window into everyday convict life. Wheelchair access to ground floor only.

☉ MUSEUM OF SYDNEY

☎ 9251 5988; www.hht.net.au; cnr Bridge & Phillip Sts; admission $10/5; ☼ 9.30am-5pm; ⓜ ⓜ ⓜ Circular Quay

Built on the site of Sydney's first (and infamously pungent) Government House, this fragmented,

storytelling museum uses state-of-the-art installations to explore the city's people, places, cultures and evolution. Indigenous origins are highlighted, evoking a poetic sense of place. Wheelchair access to ground floor only.

☉ PARLIAMENT HOUSE

☎ 9230 2111; www.parliament.nsw .gov.au; Macquarie St; admission free; ☼ 9am-5pm Mon-Fri; ⓜ Martin Place

Twinned with the Mint building further up Macquarie St, the deep veranda, formal colonnade and ochre tones of Parliament House (1816) define the world's oldest continuously operating parliamentary building. You can watch the elected representatives outdo each other on days when parliament sits. Wheelchair access by private arrangement.

☉ ROYAL BOTANIC GARDENS

☎ 9231 8111, Aboriginal Heritage Tours 9231 8134; www.rbgsyd.gov.au; Mrs Macquaries Rd; admission free, Tropical Centre $4.40/2.20; ☼ 7am-sunset, Tropical Centre 10am-4pm; ⓜ Circular Quay, Martin Place ⓜ ⓜ Circular Quay; ♿

Free guided walks start at 10.30am daily, plus 1pm from Monday to Friday. Aboriginal Heritage Tours ($20 per person) depart at 2pm on Friday. There's also a dynamic educational programme of talks and tours,

NEIGHBOURHOODS

CITY CENTRE

BATS OUT OF HELL

Cast an eye to the Sydney dusk sky, particularly around the Royal Botanic Gardens, and you'll likely see the silent spectral swoop of a fruit bat on the wing. Actually, calling them bats is a misnomer – they're grey-headed flying foxes (Pteropus policephalus), nocturnal mammals who roost in vast, chattering colonies. Vampire-esque 1m wingspans can make the blood run cold, but don't fret, they'd rather suck on a fig than your jugular.

obsessed with dirt and things that grow in it. Recent highlights have included 'Trees Worth Shouting About' and 'Superscience' sessions. Check the website for details. See also p17.

ST JAMES' CHURCH

☎ 9232 3022; www.stjameschurchsyd ney.org.au; 173 King St; admission free; 🕑 8am-6pm Mon-Fri, to 4pm Sat, 7am-4pm Sun, free tours 2.30pm Mon-Fri; 🚊 St James 🅼 City Centre

Built from convict bricks, Sydney's oldest church (1819) is another Francis Greenway extravaganza. Originally designed as a court-house, the brief changed: 'Hey Frank, we need a church!'. The cells became the crypt. Check out the balcony, sparkling copper dome, crypt shop and cool contemporary stained-glass 'Creation Window'.

SPEAKERS' CORNER

Art Gallery Rd, The Domain; admission free; 🕑 noon-4pm Sun; 🚊 St James 🚌 441; ♿

Recline on a patch of lawn in front of the Art Gallery of NSW and listen to religious zealots, nutters, political extremists, homophobes, hippies and academics express their earnest opinions. Some of them have something interesting to say; most of them are just plain mad. Either way, it makes for an interesting afternoon. BYO soapbox.

SYDNEY TOWER & SKYWALK

☎ 9333 9222; www.sydneytower.com .au, www.skywalk.com.au; 100 Market St; admission $24/18, Skywalk $109-139; 🕑 9am-10.30pm, Skywalk to 10pm; 🚊 St James 🅼 City Centre; ♿

Sydney Tower is as high as Sydneysiders get without wings or drugs – the 250m-high, 360-degree views are unbeatable. On a clear day you'll see west to the Blue Mountains, south to Botany Bay, east across the harbour to the silvery Pacific and down onto the city streets. Watch rain squalls shift across the suburbs on a stormy day. The tower also has two excellent revolving restaurants – sit and spin above the twinkling harbour city.

Luke Skywalker aspirations? The latest addition to Sydney's big-

Get high on the Sydney Skywalk

ticket tourist checklist is Skywalk: don a spiffy 'skysuit', shackle yourself to the safety rail and step onto two glass-floored viewing platforms outside Sydney Tower's observation deck, high above the street. No place for the weak-bowelled…

WATTERS GALLERY
☎ 9331 2556; www.wattersgallery .com; 109 Riley St, East Sydney; admission free; ◷ 10am-5pm Tue & Sat, 10am-7pm Wed-Fri; 🚇 Museum 🚌 389

Since 1964 this funky institution in the seamy lower reaches of Riley St has been pumping out quality. James Gleeson, Ken Whisson, Tony Tuckson and reformed rock-star Reg Mombassa are just a handful of the iconic Australian artists it holds up to the light.

🛍 SHOP
🏷 DAVID JONES
Department store
☎ 9266 5544; www.davidjones.com .au; cnr Market & Castlereagh Sts; ◷ 9.30am-6pm Mon-Fri, to 9pm Thu, 9am-6pm Sat, 10am-6pm Sun; 🚇 St James, Town Hall Ⓜ City Centre 🚌 George St buses

In two enormous city buildings, DJs is Sydney's premier department store. The Castlereagh St store has women's and children's wear and a friendly concierge to point you in the right direction. Market St has menswear, electrical and a high-brow food court: noses assail chunks of cheese, eyes flutter over antipasto, mouths drool over pastries… Your hip pocket mightn't be as keen on the whole deal as your senses.

HOBBYCO *Toy shop*
☎ 9221 0666; www.hobbyco.com.au; Shop 402, Gallery Level, Mid City Centre, Pitt St Mall; 🕑 9am-6pm Mon-Sat, to 9pm Thu, 11am-5pm Sun; 🚆 St James, Town Hall Ⓜ City Centre 🚌 George St buses

Run by hobbyists for people who take toys seriously, Hobbyco's aisles fill with excited boys (big and small) effusing over slot cars, Meccano sets, Hornby trains and radio-controlled cars (like the kick-arse Audi TT). First Fleet models and 12,000-piece jigsaw puzzles are perfect projects for a rainy year.

KINOKUNIYA *Bookshop*
☎ 9262 7996; www.kinokuniya.com; L2, The Galeries Victoria, 500 George St; 🕑 10am-7pm Mon-Sat, to 9pm Thu, 10am-6pm Sun; 🚆 Town Hall Ⓜ Galeries Victoria 🚌 George St buses

Wrapping around the Galeries Victoria atrium, Kinokuniya has over 300,000 titles – the largest bookstore in Sydney. The comics section is a magnet for geeky teens; the imported Chinese, Japanese and European magazine section isn't. Peruse the music and architecture shelves then hit the café.

LOVE & HATRED *Jewellery*
☎ 9233 3441; www.loveandhatred .com.au; L1, Strand Arcade, 412 George St; 🕑 10am-5.30pm Mon-Fri, to 8pm Thu, to 4.30pm Sat; 🚆 Town Hall Ⓜ City Centre 🚌 George St buses

This plush, sensual, wood-panelled store is aglow with custom-made jewellery by Sydney designer Giovanni D'ercole. Beautiful sapphire rings, natural pearls and rose-gold pieces manifest an unostentatious, mystic blend of Celtic, Art Nouveau and contemporary styles.

MARCS *Fashion*
☎ 9221 5575; www.marcs.com.au; Shop 228, Pitt St Mall; 🕑 9.30am-6pm Mon-Sat, to 9pm Thu, 11am-5pm Sun; 🚆 St James, Town Hall Ⓜ City Centre 🚌 George St buses

Prominent and perfect on the Pitt St Mall, Marcs' delightfully aerated boy-staff will giggle you into directional UK and Euro labels if your pocket can stand the heat. Otherwise, their own hip line of T-shirts, pants and suits won't break the bank.

NEIGHBOURHOODS

CITY CENTRE

🏬 MYER *Department store*
☎ 9238 9111; www.colesmyer.com.au; cnr George & Market Sts; ⏱ 9am-6pm Mon-Sat, to 9pm Thu, 10am-6pm Sun; 🚊 Town Hall Ⓜ City Centre 🚌 George St buses

Formerly the dowdy Grace Bros, Myer has made a concerted effort to liven things up a bit. Over seven floors, there's everything from hip fashions (Wayne Cooper, Seduce, Chloe) to big-name cosmetics (Chanel, Lancôme, Clinique), plus lingerie, sunglasses and a café.

🏬 OROTON *Fashion*
☎ 9223 2449; www.oroton.com.au; Shop 1a, 183 Pitt St Mall; ⏱ 9am-6pm Mon-Fri, to 9pm Thu, 11am-5pm Sat; 🚊 St James, Martin Place Ⓜ City Centre 🚌 George St buses

Oroton sells sophisticated leathers in a select palette of colours: black, red and tan. Wallets, handbags, belts, shoes, cufflinks and Jackie O–style sunglasses all have the air of instant classics.

🏬 PASPALEY PEARLS *Jewellery*
☎ 9232 7633; www.paspaley.com.au; 142 King St; ⏱ 9.30am-6pm Mon-Fri, 11am-5pm Sat; 🚊 St James, Martin Place Ⓜ City Centre 🚌 George St buses

This shell-shaped store sells lustrous pearls farmed along un-inhabited coastline from Darwin to Dampier in Western Australia. Classic and modern designs start at $450 for a ring, rising to more than $1 million for a hefty strand of perfect pink pearls.

🏬 QUEEN VICTORIA BUILDING *Shopping centre*
☎ 9265 6869; www.qvb.com.au; 455 George St; ⏱ 9am-6pm Mon-Sat, to 9pm Thu, 11am-5pm Sun; 🚊 Town Hall Ⓜ Galeries Victoria 🚌 George St buses

The QVB is a high-Victorian masterpiece occupying an entire city block. Yeah, sure, the 200 speciality shops are great, but check out the wrought-iron balconies, stained-glass shopfronts, mosaic floors, tinkling Baby Grand and hyper-kitsch animated Royal Clock (featuring the Battle of Hastings and hourly beheading of King Charles I).

🏬 RED EYE RECORDS *Music*
☎ 9299 4233; www.redeye.com.au; 370 Pitt St; ⏱ 9am-6pm Mon-Fri, to 9pm Thu, to 5pm Sat, 11am-5pm Sun; 🚊 Museum Ⓜ World Square 🚌 George St buses

Walking into this red-walled rock 'n' roll refuge is like waking up inside a huge, hung-over eyeball. The shelves are stocked with a rampaging collection of classic, rare and collectable records, crass rock t-shirts, books, posters and music DVDs. New music is at the 66 King St branch. Rock-on!

Shop 'til you drop in the elegant Strand Arcade

RM WILLIAMS *Australiana*
☎ 9262 2228; www.rmwilliams.com.au;
389 George St; ⌚ 8.30am-6pm Mon-Fri,
to 8.30pm Thu, 9am-5pm Sat, 11am-5pm
Sun; 🚊 Town Hall Ⓜ City Centre
🚌 George St buses

Urban cowboys and country folk
can't get enough of this hard-
wearing outback gear. It's the
kind of stuff politicians don when
they want to seem 'fair dinkum'
about something. Prime ministerial
favourites include oilskin jackets,
Akubra hats, moleskin jeans and
leatherwork boots.

STRAND ARCADE
Shopping centre
☎ 9232 4199; www.strandarcade.com
.au; 412 George St & 193-5 Pitt St Mall;
⌚ 7.30am-6pm Mon-Sat, to 9pm Thu,
10am-5pm Sun; 🚊 Town Hall Ⓜ City
Centre 🚌 George St buses

Constructed in 1891 in a squeezy
space between George and Pitt Sts,
the Strand Arcade rivals the QVB in
the ornateness stakes. Three floors
of designer fashions, Australiana
and old-world coffee shops are
guaranteed to make your short cut
through here considerably longer.

ALL THAT GLITTERS

Downtown Sydney is a hotspot for stand-out jewellers, comin' atcha like Cleopatra:

> **Fairfax & Roberts** (☎ 9232 8511; www.fairfaxandroberts.com.au; 44 Martin Pl;
  ⏱ 10am-6pm Mon-Fri, to 8.30pm Thu, 10.30am-4pm Sat; 🚆 Martin Place) Classy,
  classy, classy... A night at the opera?

> **Martin & Stein** (☎ 9267 6628; www.martinandstein.com.au; Shop 26, QVB, 455 George
  St; ⏱ 10am-5pm Mon-Sat, to 9pm Thu, 11am-5pm Sun; 🚆 Town Hall Ⓜ Galeries
  Victoria 🚌 George St buses) Objects of virtue, antique jewellery and high security.

> **Tiffany & Co** (☎ 9235 1777; www.tiffany.com; 28 Castlereagh St; ⏱ 10am-5pm
  Mon-Sat, to 7pm Thu, noon-4pm Sun; 🚆 Martin Place) Gorgeous glitterati and serious
  rocks.

Milling around the balconies on level one, top Australian designers commune and collude. Release your inner vixen in low-cut, butt-hugger jeans from **Bettina Liano** (www.bettinaliano.com.au), devilishly daring gear from **Wayne Cooper** (www.waynecooper.com.au), Sydney's best swimwear, hats and suits from **Zimmermann** (www.zimmermannwear.com), and fishnets and flounce from **Alannah Hill** (www.alannahhill.com.au).

🏛 STRAND HATTERS
Australiana

☎ 9231 6884; www.strandhatters.com.au; Strand Arcade, 412 George St; ⏱ 8.30am-6pm Mon-Fri, to 8pm Thu, 9.30am-4.30pm Sat, 10am-5pm Sun; 🚆 Town Hall Ⓜ City Centre 🚌 George St buses

Got a cold/wet head? Strand Hatters will cover your crown with a classically Australian Akubra bush hat (made from rabbit felt), a beret, bowler or a Monte Cristo 'Gambler' panama. Staff will block and steam hats to customer requirements (crocodile-teeth hatbands cost extra).

🏛 WORLD SQUARE
Shopping centre

☎ 9262 7926; www.worldsquare.com.au; cnr George & Liverpool Sts; ⏱ 10am-7pm Mon-Sat, to 9pm Thu, 11am-5pm Sun; 🚆 Town Hall Ⓜ World Square 🚌 George St buses

The old Anthony Horden & Sons department store on this site was demolished in the '80s, and it's taken 20 years for World Square to emerge in its place. City-slickers have been rewarded for their patience with coffee shops, sushi bars, a supermarket, shoe stores and a huge Rebel Sport outlet for every conceivable bat, ball or racket.

🍴 EAT

🍴 BAR REGGIO *Italian* $$

☎ 9332 1129; fax 9332 1129; 135 Crown St, East Sydney; ⏰ 10am-11pm Mon-Fri, to midnight Sat; 🚇 Museum 🚌 389

Blink and you'll miss this classic little dim-lit Italian diner in East Sydney's 'Little Italy' district, a short walk from the CBD. The walls are plastered with Ferrari flags and Rome murals; the menu board in the window has been there so long the lettering has started to flake off. Pasta, pizza, meat and fish dishes have stood the test of time. Closed Sundays (church!).

🍴 BÉCASSE *French* $$$

☎ 9283 3440; www.becasse.com.au; 204 Clarence St; ⏰ noon-2.30pm Tue-Fri, 6-10.30pm Tue-Sat; 🚇 Town Hall 🚇 Galeries Victoria 🚌 George St buses

There's nothing gratuitously flashy about Bécasse, but it will linger as one of the most memorable dining experiences of your trip, the muted, elegant décor perfectly complementing superbly created dishes. The Degustation Menu ($110) is 10 courses of gustatory heaven. Wines by the glass; reservations essential.

🍴 BODHI *Chinese/Vegan* $$

☎ 9360 2523; bodhibar@three.com .au; Cook & Phillip Park, 2-4 College St; ⏰ 10am-11pm Tue-Sun, to 4pm Mon, yum cha 10am-4pm daily; 🚇 Museum, St James; ♿ Ⓥ ♿

Bodhi scores highly for its cool design and leafy position. Quick-fire waiters bounce off stainless-steel minimalism inside and slatted wooden tables and umbrellas outside. Have a swim at the pool next door before daily yum cha, a relaxed and value-for-money affair. The barbeque buns rule.

🍴 EST. *Mod Oz* $$$$

☎ 9240 3010; www.merivale.com; L1, Establishment Hotel, 252 George St; ⏰ noon-2.30pm & 6-10pm Mon-Fri, 6-10pm Sat; 🚇 Circular Quay, Wynyard 🚌 🚢 Circular Quay; ♿

Pressed-tin ceilings, huge columns, oversize windows and modern furniture make Est. a must-see for the interior design as much as the food. Menu stunners include scallops with sauternes and carrot emulsion, and baked baby barramundi. Zealous wine attendants will fetch your desired champagne from the cellar.

🍴 FORTY ONE *Mod Oz* $$$

☎ 9221 2500; www.forty-one.com .au; L42, Chifley Tower, 2 Chifley Sq; ⏰ noon-3pm Tue-Fri, 6-10pm Mon-Sat; 🚇 Martin Place 🚌 George St buses; ♿

Luxury dining with harbour sights and lights – the view extends forever, but the mood remains strangely intimate. It's actually on the 42nd floor, but at this rarefied altitude, most folks are too oxygen-deprived to worry about such details.

🍴 MOTHER CHU'S VEGETARIAN KITCHEN
Vegetarian $

☎ 9283 2828; www.motherchusveget arian.com.au; 367 Pitt St; 🕑 noon-3pm & 6-10pm Mon-Sat; 🚈 Museum Ⓜ World Square 🚌 George St buses; Ⓥ 🚻

Shimmering in plastique splendour beneath the monorail, Mother Chu's blends vegetarian Taiwanese, Japanese and Chinese influences to ensure the perfect tofu or claypot hit. There's not much going on in terms of ambience, but the veg-lovers don't seem to mind.

🍴 PRIME *Steakhouse* $$$

☎ 9229 7777; www.gposydney.com; LG, GPO Bldg, 1 Martin Pl; 🕑 noon-3pm Mon-Fri, 6-10pm Mon-Sat; 🚈 Martin Place 🚌 George St buses; ♿

Need a massive shot of iron? Venture into this carnivores' paradise, deep in a dark, subterranean sandstone bunker. The succulent 400g, aged rib-eye with silky potato purée and a red wine sauce is a protein-packed knockout.

🍴 TETSUYA'S
French/Japanese $$$$

☎ 9267 2900; www.tetsuyas.com; 529 Kent St; 🕑 noon-1.30pm Sat, 6.30-9pm Tue-Sat; 🚈 Town Hall Ⓜ World Square 🚌 George St buses

Down a clandestine security driveway, Tetsuya's could well be the ultimate dining experience. Japanese-born Tetsuya Wakuda creates morsels of fusion food with lashings of flavour. You'll find a perfect match for the confit of ocean trout in the 3000-bottle wine cellar. Book way ahead.

🍸 DRINK

🍸 ARTHOUSE *Pub*

☎ 9284 1200; www.thearthousehotel .com.au; 275 Pitt St; admission free; 🕑 11am-midnight Mon-Wed, to 1am Thu, to 3am Fri, 5pm-6am Sat; 🚈 Town Hall Ⓜ Galeries Victoria 🚌 George St buses; ♿

It's easy to lose your way in here, pinballing between three cool bars and Dome restaurant, staggering through doorways into live jazz performances, dance parties or life-drawing sessions. After-work punters seem to know their way around – follow someone good-looking.

🍸 BAR EUROPA *Bar*

☎ 9232 3377; www.bareuropa.com .au; Basement, 88 Elizabeth St; admission free; 🕑 4pm-late Tue-Fri, 8pm-late Sat; 🚈 Martin Place Ⓜ City Centre

Basement vibe, subtle lighting, DJs spinning laid-back funk and three debonair rooms divided by sexy screens cement Europa's reputation as an intimate, clubby hideaway for inner-city professionals. Sip a 'Sydneysider Sour', sigh, and wonder what he/she is doing now…

☿ BAVARIAN BIER CAFÉ
Beer café

☎ 8297 4155; www.bavarianbiercafe .com.au; 24 York St; admission free; ☾ 10am-late Mon-Fri, 11am-late Sat; 🚇 Museum Ⓜ World Square 🚌 George St buses

Stepping in the door of this café you'll feel like you've put your head inside an enormous chandelier – sparkling racks of steins dangle above the central bar, waiting for you to fill them with litres of Löwenbrau. Soak it all up with some bratwurst, sauerkraut and a pretzel at the long *bierhalle* tables.

☿ ESTABLISHMENT *Bar*

☎ 9240 3000; www.merivale.com; 252 George St; admission free; ☾ 11am-late Mon-Fri, 6pm-late Sat; 🚇 Circular Quay, Wynyard 🚌 🚢 Circular Quay; ♿

Establishment's cashed-up crush proves the art of swilling cocktails after a hard, city day is not lost. Sit at the majestic marble bar, in the swish courtyard or be absorbed by a leather lounge as stockbrokers scribble their phone numbers on

the backs of coasters for flirty city chicks.

☿ HEMMESPHERE *Bar*

☎ 9240 3040; www.merivale.com; L4, Establishment Hotel, 252 George St; admission free; ☾ 6pm-2am Tue & Wed, noon-3am Thu & Fri, 7pm-late Sat; 🚇 Circular Quay, Wynyard 🚌 🚢 Circular Quay; ♿

This mature, private lounge is pure Sydney opulence; a lush gentlemen's-club vibe peppered with Moroccan twists. Melt into a deep, leather chair, order a cigar and mandarin caipiroska and wait for someone famous to show up. Bookings essential.

☿ ORBIT BAR *Bar*

☎ 9247 9777; www.summitrestaurant .com.au; L47, The Summit, Australia Sq; admission free; ☾ 5pm-late; 🚇 Wynyard 🚌 George St buses; ♿

A murderously cool, revolving *Goldfinger*-esque bar, orbiting your mind with killer cocktails and views to-die-for. Try the 'D'lux': fresh lychees pureed and shaken silly with Grey Goose orange vodka and Grand Marnier.

☿ REDOAK *Beer café*

☎ 9262 3303; www.redoak.com.au; 201 Clarence St; admission free; ☾ 11am-10.30pm Mon-Wed, to 1am Thu-Sat; 🚇 Town Hall Ⓜ Darling Park

With over 20 handmade beers available, this place should keep you

IMPORTANT BEER INFORMATION

Beer in Sydney comes in three glass sizes. Traditional Australian pubs serve the heavenly golden nectar in middys (285mL) and schooners (425mL). Pints (570mL) are the domain of the countless Anglo-Celtic theme pubs that have slipped through quarantine recently. Australian pubs abandoned pints centuries ago because beer would go warm in the summer heat before you'd finished your glass. Arm yourself with this invaluable local insight and order a schooner instead.

off the streets for a while. Pull up a stool among the international crew and work your way through the much-awarded list. If things start to slip away from you, slow your descent with the excellent bar food.

☑ TANK STREAM BAR *Bar*

☎ 9240 3000; www.merivale.com; 1 Tank Stream Way; admission free; ⏰ 4pm-midnight Mon-Fri, from noon Fri; 🚉 Circular Quay, Wynyard 🚌 🚢 Circular Quay; ♿

After-work suits and secretaries get high and heady poised over Sydney's original water supply. The Tank Stream runs thick with bottled beer, wine and cocktails, and the corporate mob can't get enough. Neither could Robbie Williams.

☑ ZETA *Bar*

☎ 9265 6070; www.zetabar.com .au; L4, Hilton Hotel, 488 George St; admission free; ⏰ 5pm-2am Mon-Fri, to 3.30am Sat; 🚉 St James Ⓜ City Centre 🚌 George St buses; ♿

Ride the Hilton escalators up to Zeta, which captivates a chic

young city crew with its white vinyl lounges, discrete curtained booths (what *was* Snoop Dogg smoking in there?) and enormous gas inferno. Here you can sip grilled-fruit cocktails and eyeball the QVB dome from the terrace.

PLAY

☆ CITY RECITAL HALL

Live music

☎ 8256 2222; www.cityrecitalhall .com; 2-12 Angel Pl; tickets free-$60; ⏰ box office 9am-5pm Mon-Fri; 🚉 Martin Place, Wynyard Ⓜ City Centre 🚌 George St buses; ♿

Based on the classical configuration of the 19th-century European concert hall, the custom-built 1200-seat City Recital Hall boasts near-perfect acoustics. Catch top-flight companies like Musica Viva, the Australian Brandenburg and Chamber Orchestras and the Sydney Symphony as well as touring

Sydney Philharmonia Motet Choir entertain at the City Recital Hall

international ensembles, soloists and opera singers.

⭐ CONSERVATORIUM OF MUSIC *Live music*

☎ 9351 2222; www.music.usyd.edu.au; cnr Macquarie & Bridge Sts; tickets free-$25; ⏰ box office 9am-5pm Mon-Fri; 🚉 Circular Quay, Martin Place 🚌 🚊 Circular Quay; ♿

'The Con' has a history of bulbous building costs: $145 million was spent recently to refurbish its five venues. The annual student/teacher performance programme includes choral, jazz, operatic and chamber recitals and free lunch-time and 'Cocktail Hour' concerts.

⭐ METRO *Live music*

☎ 9287 2000; www.metrotheatre.com.au; 624 George St; tickets $25-65; ⏰ box office 10am-7pm Mon-Fri, noon-7pm Sat; 🚉 Town Hall Ⓜ City Centre 🚌 George St buses; ♿

The Metro must be a frontrunner for the 'Sydney's Rockingest Rock Venue' trophy. Big-name indie acts like The Eels, well-chosen local acts like The Butterfly Effect, and international DJs lend weight to the cause. Theatre-style tiers, air-con, super sound and visibility: r-o-c-k ROCK!

⭐ SYDNEY ARCHITECTURE WALKS *Organised tour*

☎ 8239 2211; www.sydneyarchitecture.org; tours depart Museum of Sydney, cnr Bridge & Phillip Sts; tours $25; ⏰ 2hr walks, rain or shine

Whoa, who designed *that* gorgeous hacienda/heinous behemoth? These bright young archi-buffs run four themed walking tours: Sydney Opera House, Public Art, Harbour Features & Buildings and Urban Patterns of Sydney. Call for bookings and departure times.

⭐ TANK *Club*
☎ 9240 3007; www.tankclub.com.au; 3 Bridge La; admission Fri/Sat $15/25; 🕙 10pm–6am Fri & Sat; 🚆 🚌 🚢 Circular Quay

They've got a VIP room – the question is, are you 'I' enough? Muster tank-loads of glamour and buckets of chutzpah and crash the party. Otherwise, mingle with *waaay*-too-young, clean-shaven stockbrokers and their waif girlfriends in this world-class, underground club.

⭐ WINE BANQ *Live music*
☎ 9222 1919; www.winebanq.com.au; 53 Martin Pl; admission from $10; 🕙 noon–late Tue–Fri, 6pm–late Sat; 🚆 Martin Place Ⓜ City Centre

Hands down, this is the sexiest jazz room in Sydney. The whole place looks like it was carved out of an architect's book of dreams; a brilliant wine list only adds to the appeal. Past performers include Wynton Marsalis, James Morrison and Harry Connick Jr.

>THE ROCKS & CIRCULAR QUAY

Sydney's original European settlement clung to the rocky shelves of The Rocks (www.therocks.com). It was a seedy place, where sailors, whalers and rapscallions boozed and brawled shamelessly in countless harbourside pubs. These days The Rocks is sanitised, touristy and prepackaged, but (thankfully) the historic atmosphere is undeniable. It's an interesting place to wander around for an afternoon, as are Observatory Hill and Millers Point, flanking the western side of the Sydney Harbour Bridge. Sydney's most esteemed theatre and dance companies congregate around Walsh Bay on The Rocks' northern fringe. For more on The Rocks, see p16.

Circular Quay is Sydney's transport hub. The air quality is pretty dire beneath the freeway and railway lines, but around Sydney Cove are some of the city's most esteemed restaurants and, of course, the Sydney Opera House (as if you could miss it). Also here are some impressive museums and galleries, and more bad buskers than you can throw a 5¢ coin at.

THE ROCKS & CIRCULAR QUAY

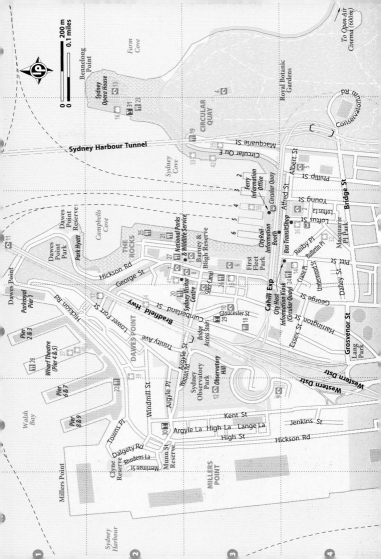

NEIGHBOURHOODS

THE ROCKS & CIRCULAR QUAY

SEE

CADMAN'S COTTAGE
☎ 9247 5033; www.npws.nsw.gov.au; 110 George St, The Rocks; admission free; ⏰ 9.30am-4.30pm Mon-Fri, 10am-4.30pm Sat & Sun; 🚲 🚌 🚢 Circular Quay
Built on a buried beach, Cadman's Cottage is Sydney's oldest house (1816). Namesake John Cadman was Government Coxswain (boat and crew superintendent). Water Police detained criminals here in the 1840s; it was later converted into a home for retired sea captains.

CUSTOMS HOUSE
☎ 9242 8555; www.cityofsydney.nsw.gov.au/library; 31 Alfred St, Circular Quay; admission free; ⏰ 8am-midnight Mon-Fri, 10am-midnight Sat, noon-5pm Sun; 🚲 🚌 🚢 Circular Quay; ♿
Emerging phoenixlike from extensive renovations, this cavernous harbourside construction (1885) now houses the Customs House Library. Under the glass lobby floor is a charmingly geeky 1:500 model of Sydney; the slick Café Sydney (p56) is on the roof.

GANNON HOUSE
☎ 9251 4474; www.gannonhousegallery.com; 45 Argyle St, The Rocks; admission free; ⏰ 10am-6.30pm; 🚲 🚌 🚢 Circular Quay
Purchasing works directly from aboriginal communities, Gannon House (named after colonial builder Michael Gannon) takes an umbrella approach to its gallery exhibits, jumbling Aboriginal artefacts, paintings and didgeridoos with contemporary white Australian abstract art. The results are surprisingly harmonious.

GOVERNMENT HOUSE
☎ 9931 5222; www.hht.net.au; admission free; ⏰ 10am-3pm Fri-Sun, grounds to 4pm daily; 🚲 Circular Quay, Martin Place 🚌 🚢 Circular Quay
Encased in English-style grounds within the Royal Botanic Gardens (p35), this Gothic sandstone mansion has sensational harbour views. Unless there's an event happening, you can tour through the fussy furnishings – look for paintings by Streeton, Roberts and Drysdale.

JUSTICE & POLICE MUSEUM
☎ 9252 1144; www.hht.net.au; cnr Albert & Phillip Sts, Circular Quay; admission $8/4; ⏰ 10am-5pm Sat & Sun, daily in Jan, group bookings Mon-Fri; 🚲 🚌 🚢 Circular Quay
In the old Water Police Station (1858), this museum adopts the guise of a late-19th-century police station and court. Focussing on disreputable activities, exhibits include confiscated weapons, butt-ugly mugshots and forensic evidence from Sydney's most heinous crimes. Wheelchair access to ground floor only.

WORTH THE TRIP

Across the Sydney Harbour Bridge from The Rocks is the famous 1935 amusement park **Luna Park** (☎ 9922 6644; www.lunaparksydney.com; 1 Olympic Pl, Milsons Point; admission free, multiride passes from $20; 🕙 10am-10pm Sun-Thu, to midnight Fri & Sat; 🚇 🚊 Milsons Point; 🚻) with its sinister chip-toothed clown entry. The park has been periodically closed by noise police in recent decades – get in now before it closes again! The Ferris Wheel, Rotor, Flying Saucer and Tumble Bug offer varying degrees of nerve-wrack and nausea.

◉ MUSEUM OF CONTEMPORARY ART

☎ 9245 2400; www.mca.com.au; 140 George St, Circular Quay; admission free; 🕙 10am-5pm; 🚌 🚆 🚊 Circular Quay; 🚻

In a harbourside Art Deco edifice, the MCA has been raising even the most open-minded Sydney eyebrows since 1991. Constantly changing controversial exhibitions from Australia and overseas range from incredibly hip to in-your-face, sexually explicit and profoundly disturbing. Impressive.

◉ ORIGINAL & AUTHENTIC ABORIGINAL ART

☎ 9251 4222; www.authaboriginalart.com.au; 79 George St, The Rocks; admission free; 🕙 10am-6pm; 🚌 🚆 🚊 Circular Quay

This trustworthy gallery specialises in works from four specific regions – the Central and Western Deserts, Queensland, Arnhem Land and the Kimberleys – with info available on the artists, and some more unusual stuff for sale like painted

glass and traditional sand paintings preserved on canvas.

◉ ROCKS DISCOVERY MUSEUM

☎ 1800 067 676; www.rocksdiscoverymuseum.com; 2-8 Kendall La, The Rocks; admission free; 🕙 10am-5pm; 🚌 🚆 🚊 Circular Quay

Divided into four chronological displays (pre-1788, 1788–1820, 1820–1900 and 1900-present) this excellent new museum digs deep into Rocks history and leads you on an artefact-soaked tour. Sensitive attention is given to The Rocks' original inhabitants, the Cadigal people. Wheelchair access to ground floor only.

◉ SH ERVIN GALLERY

☎ 9258 0173; www.nsw.nationaltrust.org.au/ervin.html; National Trust Centre, Observatory Hill, Watson Rd, The Rocks; admission $6/4; 🕙 11am-5pm Tue-Sun; 🚆 🚊 Circular Quay 🚌 339, 431-4; 🚻

High on the hill inside a former military hospital and high school, the SH Ervin Gallery exhibits invariably rewarding historical and contemporary Australian art. Annual mainstays include the 'Salon des Refuses' (alternative Archibald Prize entries), 'The Year in Art' and the 'Portia Geach Memorial Award'.

SUSANNAH PLACE

☎ 9241 1893; fax 9241 2608; 58-64 Gloucester St, The Rocks; admission $8/4; 🕑 10am-5pm Sat & Sun, daily Jan; 🚇 🚌 🛳 Circular Quay

Dating from 1844, the typically claustrophobic Susannah Place is a diminutive terrace of tiny houses with a tiny shop selling tiny historical wares. My, haven't we grown?

SYDNEY HARBOUR BRIDGE

☎ 9240 1100; www.pylonlookout.com .au; museum admission $9/3.50; 🕑 10am-5pm; 🚇 🚌 🛳 Circular Quay, Milsons Point

Climb the 200 stairs inside the southeast pylon of the iconic Sydney Harbour Bridge (see p11) and check out the museum. Three levels of exhibits focus on the bridge's planning and construction, and the uncompromising vision of chief engineer JJC Bradfield. And the view is pretty sweet! The entrance is on the pedestrian walkway across the bridge, accessed via the stairs from Cumberland St, The Rocks, or Milsons Point train station, on the north shore. If you'd like to

COAT-HANGER COMPENDIUM

Out-nerd your mates with a fistful of Harbour Bridge stats:

> The old coat-hanger is 134m high, 502m long and 49m wide
> 1400 workers took nine years to build it
> 16 builders died in construction accidents
> A full makeover takes 10 years and 30,000L of paint
> It weighs nearly 53,000 tonnes
> Six million bolts hold it together; a mythical solid-gold rivet somewhere on the bridge remains elusive

clamber on the bridge itself, see BridgeClimb, p60.

SYDNEY OBSERVATORY

☎ 9217 0485; www.sydneyobservatory .com.au; Observatory Hill, Watson Rd, The Rocks; admission free, 3-D Space Theatre $7/5, Night Viewings $15/12; 🕑 10am-5pm, 3-D Space Theatre 2.30 & 3.30pm Mon-Fri, 11am, noon, 2.30 & 3.30pm Sat & Sun; 🚇 🛳 Circular Quay 🚌 339, 431-4

Built in the 1850s, Sydney's copper-domed, Italianate observatory squats atop Observatory Hill. Inside is Australia's oldest working telescope (1874), a 3-D Space Theatre and an interactive Australian Astronomy exhibition of Aboriginal sky stories and modern stargazing. Squint at galaxies far, far away during Night Viewings

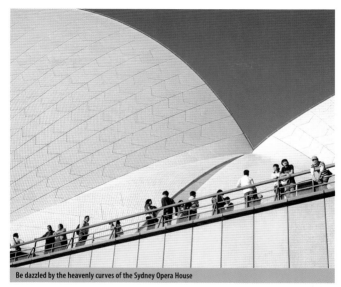
Be dazzled by the heavenly curves of the Sydney Opera House

(bookings required). If you're feeling more earthly, Observatory Park is great for a terrestrial picnic.

⊙ SYDNEY OPERA HOUSE

☎ 9250 7111, box office 9250 7777, tours 9250 7250; www.sydneyopera house.com; Bennelong Pt, Circular Quay East; building admission free, performances $25-220; ⊙ box office 9am-8.30pm Mon-Sat, 2hr preshow Sun; 🚇 🚌 ⛴ Circular Quay; ♿
A one-hour tour of Sydney's fabulous Opera House costs

$26 for adults, $18 concession, departing half-hourly from 9am to 5pm. Unless there are rehearsals underway, you can see most things behind-the-scenes. Also running is the 'Kids at the House' programme, featuring kids' music, dance and drama including introductory ballet with Australian Ballet dancers. The free bimonthly *Events* diary has upcoming listings; the Sydney Opera House Market (p54) happens on Sunday. See also p10, and p62 for entertainment options.

SHOP

⬠ AUSTRALIAN WINE CENTRE
Food & drink

☎ 9247 2755; www.australianwinecen
tre.com; Shop 3, Goldfields House,
1 Alfred St, Circular Quay; ⏱ 9.30am-
7pm Mon-Wed & Sat, to 8pm Thu & Fri, to
6.30pm Sun; 🚈 🚌 🚢 Circular Quay

Shop beneath the sails at The Rocks Market

This multilingual basement store
is packed full of quality Australian wine, beer and spirits. Pick
up some Yellowglen for a bubbly
night or organise a shipment
of Ninth Island Pinot Noir back
home. Healthy wallets can
access Cuban cigars and a swag-
gering range of Penfolds Grange
wines.

⬠ DONE ART & DESIGN
Australiana

☎ 9251 6099; www.done.com.au;
123-5 George St, The Rocks; ⏱ 10am-
6pm; 🚈 🚌 🚢 Circular Quay
Ken Done is like George Michael –
he peaked in the '80s but he just
won't go away. The sunny side
of Australiana, his optimistic,
colourful images of Sydney icons
are primed for the tourist market.
They're emblazoned on everything from t-shirts to handbags.
Strewth Ken, not another Opera
House mouse-pad…

⬠ SYDNEY OPERA HOUSE
MARKET *Market*

☎ 9315 7011; www.blueskymarkets
.com.au/soh.html; Sydney Opera House,
Bennelong Pt, Circular Quay East;
⏱ 9am-4pm Sun; 🚈 🚌 🚢 Circular
Quay
Under big, cream umbrellas and
Opera House arcs, elbow for position in the hunt for high-quality
contemporary Australian ceramics,

gems, toys, jewellery, hats, paintings, photographs and souvenirs. If the 40 stalls don't satisfy, just dig the architecture.

THE ROCKS MARKET *Market*
☎ 9240 8717; www.therocksmarket
.com; George St, The Rocks, near Sydney
Harbour Bridge; ☺ 10am-5pm Sat &
Sun; 🚇 🚌 🚢 Circular Quay
The promoter's line goes, 'Choose something you like, somewhere you love'. Under a long white canopy, the 150 stalls here are a little on the tacky side of the tracks (fossils, opals, faux-Aboriginal art etc) but are still worth a gander. Maybe what you choose to like will be the buskers and a beer at the pub.

🍴 EAT

🍴 ALTITUDE *Mod Oz* $$$
☎ 9250 6123; www.shangri-la.com
/sydney; L36, Shangri-La Hotel, 176
Cumberland St, The Rocks; ☺ 6pm-late
Mon-Sat; 🚇 🚌 🚢 Circular Quay; ♿
London chef Michael Kean plates up top-notch Mod Oz at Altitude, sending your taste buds soaring as high as the harbour views. If you've only got a day or two in Sydney, make this your last hurrah.

🍴 ARIA *Modern European* $$$$
☎ 9252 2555; www.ariarestaurant
.com; 1 Macquarie St, Circular Quay

WORTH THE TRIP
Perched above the North Sydney Olympic Pool just across the bridge from The Rocks is super-slick **Aqua Dining** (☎ 9964 9998; www.aquadining
.com.au; cnr Paul & Northcliff Sts, Milsons Pt; ☺ noon-2.30pm & 6-10pm; 🚌 🚢 Milsons Point; ♿ Ⓥ). Muted mushroom hues play second-fiddle to bridge and harbour views, while the service is superior – that rare mix of courteous, knowledgeable (the wine list beggars belief) and amiable. Put your hand up for the saddle of lamb.

East; ☺ noon-3pm & 5.30-11pm
Mon-Fri, 5.30-11pm Sat, 6-10pm Sun;
🚇 🚌 🚢 Circular Quay; ♿
Aria is a star in Sydney's fine-dining firmament, an award-winning combination of chef Matthew Moran's stellar dishes, awesome Opera House views (*is* there a cooler building?) and faultless service. The mouth-watering lamb rack is hard to overlook. Pre- and after-theatre supper menu available.

🍴 BEL MONDO *Italian* $$$
☎ 9241 3700; www.belmondo
.com.au; L3, Argyle Stores, Gloucester
Walk, The Rocks; ☺ 6-10pm Mon-Sat;
🚇 🚌 🚢 Circular Quay; ♿
Expect northern Italian cuisine perfectly executed by chef Grant

THE ROCKS & CIRCULAR QUAY

Lawrence in dramatic surrounds – space, views, elegance and pizzazz; *very* Sydney. For a more relaxed meal, the cool and casual bar is perfect for an after-work bite or a late-night supper.

🍴 CAFÉ SYDNEY *Mod Oz* $$$
☎ 9251 8683; www.cafesydney
.com; L5, Customs House, Circular Quay;
🕑 noon-11pm Mon-Fri, 5-11pm Sat,
noon-4pm Sun; 🚉 🚌 ⚓ Circular Quay;
♿ V ♿

A roomy dining hall on the Customs House roof with outrageous harbour views, outdoor terrace, glass ceiling, cocktail bar, friendly staff, Sunday afternoon jazz and super-chef Nino Borgo; the list of Café Sydney's pluses is as long as your arm. Seafood and wood-grilled dishes prevail.

🍴 CRUISE *Mod Oz* $$$
☎ 9251 1188; www.cruiserestaurant
.com.au; L2, Overseas Passenger Terminal, Circular Quay West; 🕑 noon-2.30pm Mon-Fri, 6-10.30pm Mon-Sat;
🚉 🚌 ⚓ Circular Quay; ♿ V

The cocktail lounge upstairs wallows in lugubrious style; the bar downstairs does a heady trade. In between, Cruise restaurant cooks up satisfying serves of prawn-and-scallop dumplings with red vinegar, and local snapper fillet with shaved fennel, prawns and tomato vinaigrette. Tasty work.

🍴 FIREFLY *Tapas/wine bar* $$
☎ 9241 2031; www.fireflybar.net;
Lot 5, Pier 7, 17 Hickson Rd, Walsh Bay,
The Rocks; 🕑 noon-11pm Mon-Sat;
🚉 ⚓ Circular Quay 🚌 430-4;
♿ V

Compact, classy and never snooty, Firefly's outdoor candlelit tables fill with pretheatre patrons having a quick meal before the show. Come after 8pm when the audience has taken its seats and toast the Walsh Bay powerboats with some fine wine.

🍴 GUILLAUME AT BENNELONG
Mod Oz/French $$$$
☎ 9241 1999; www.guillaumeatbe
nnelong.com.au; Sydney Opera House,
Bennelong Pt, Circular Quay East;
🕑 noon-3pm Thu & Fri, 5.30pm-late
Mon-Sat; 🚉 🚌 ⚓ Circular Quay;
♿ V

Turn the old 'dinner and a show' cliché into something meaningful at the Sydney Opera House. Snuggle into a banquette and enjoy acclaimed chef Guillaume Brahimi's masterful cuisine. His basil-infused tuna with mustard seed and soy vinaigrette has fans hollering operatically all over town.

🍴 ONE ALFRED STREET
Café/wine bar $$
☎ 9241 4636; onealfredst@bigpond
.com; 1 Alfred St, Circular Quay; 🕑 8am-

late, kitchen noon-9pm;
🚇 🚌 ⛴ Circular Quay; ♿ Ⓥ
An unexpected gem among
the morass of Circular Quay
fast-food joints, One Alfred
Street serves up classics like
slow-cooked Wagyu beef with
potato and parsnip flakes and
quality fish and chips. Also great
for a morning caffeine fix or a
lazy afternoon vino (Antipodean
wines only!).

🍴 QUAY *Mod Oz* $$$
☎ 9251 5600; www.quay.com.au; L3,
Overseas Passenger Terminal, Circular
Quay West; 🕑 noon-2.30pm Tue-Fri,
6-10pm daily; 🚇 🚌 ⛴ Circular Quay;
♿ Ⓥ
With iconic Sydney on view,
sitting on the balcony next to
the teary, streamer-hurling non-
embarkers at the OSPT is surreal.
Equally euphoric is Quay's stylish
service, outstanding wine list and
Peter Gilmore's cooking (try the
poached quail with truffle custard,
radish, sherry reduction and baked
milk skin).

🍴 ROCKPOOL *Mod Oz* $$$$
☎ 9252 1888; www.rockpool.com; 107
George St, The Rocks; 🕑 6-11pm Tue-
Sat; 🚇 🚌 ⛴ Circular Quay; Ⓥ
Behind an unassuming green
façade, Rockpool is arguably
Sydney's best restaurant (oh,
how they argue). Chef Neil Perry's

modern seafood creations continue to wow the critics – expect
crafty, contemporary cuisine with
Asian influences, faultless service
and an alluring wine list. Try Perry's signature stir-fried mud crab
omelette.

🍴 SAILORS THAI CANTEEN
Thai $$
☎ 9251 2466; fax 9251 2610; 106
George St, The Rocks; 🕑 noon-10pm
Mon-Sat; 🚇 🚌 ⛴ Circular Quay;
Ⓥ ♿
Wedge yourself into a gap be-
tween arts-community operators,
politicians and media manoeuvr-
ers at Sailors' long communal
table and order the Chiang Mai
chicken curry. The balcony tables
fill up fast, but fortune might be
smiling on you.

🍴 THE WHARF *Mod Oz* $$$
☎ 9250 1761; www.thewharfres
taurant.com.au; Pier 4, Hickson Rd,
Walsh Bay, The Rocks; 🕑 noon-3pm &
6pm-late Mon-Sat; 🚇 ⛴ Circular Quay
🚌 430-4
Picture-postcard views, sexy staff
and photo-worthy Mod Oz – The
Wharf has it all on tap, but man-
ages to remain unpretentious and
grounded. Perfect for a romantic
occasion (such as your holiday), or
a pre- or post-theatre drink or bite.
One of our favourites.

DRINK

AUSTRALIAN HOTEL *Pub*

☎ 9247 2229; www.australianheritage
hotel.com; 100 Cumberland St, The
Rocks; admission free; ⏰ 11am-
midnight Mon-Sat, to 10pm Sun;
🚉 🚌 🚢 Circular Quay

This laid-back, good-humoured
hotel has an astounding 96 Australian brews on offer. Try to think
of four more to hit the century as
you wobble through the list. The
pub food borders on gourmet,
and you can also sleep upstairs if
you've had a few too many.

BLU HORIZON *Bar*

☎ 9250 6000; www.shangri-la.com
/sydney; L36, Shangri-La Hotel, 176
Cumberland St, The Rocks; admission
free; ⏰ 5pm-late; 🚉 🚌 🚢 Circular
Quay; ♿

Look, George Clooney's skinny-
dipping in the Park Hyatt roof
pool! If you can tear your eyes
away, the horizon is indeed
blue, the views stretching from
here to New Zealand. Can you
believe there are 300 cocktails at
bartender Loy Catada's disposal?
Believe it.

Surround yourself with famous icons at the Opera Bar

NEIGHBOURHOODS

THE ROCKS & CIRCULAR QUAY

RESPONSIBLE SERVING OF ALCOHOL

Pub cellars at The Rocks were regularly used as impromptu holding cells for passed-out boozers. After emptying their customers' pockets, publicans would dutifully pour drunks down their coal chutes to sleep off the grog in peace. These dank sandstone pits witnessed many a foul hangover, sometimes also harbouring escaped convicts and crims on the run.

LORD NELSON BREWERY HOTEL *Pub*

☎ 9251 4044; www.lordnelson.com.au; 19 Kent St, Millers Point; admission free; ⏱ 11am-11pm Mon-Sat, noon-10pm Sun; 🚉 🚢 Circular Quay 🚌 339, 431-4
Built in 1841, the 'Nello' claims to be Sydney's oldest pub (or is it the Hero of Waterloo down the road?) The onsite brewery cooks up robust stouts and ales (try the 'Nelson's Blood') and there's decent midrange accommodation upstairs too.

OPERA BAR *Bar*

☎ 9247 1666; www.operabar.com.au; Lower Concourse, Sydney Opera House, Bennelong Pt, Circular Quay East; admission free; ⏱ 11am-late; 🚉 🚌 🚢 Circular Quay; ♿
Lapping on the harbour's edge under the low-slung Opera House eaves, this sexy, curvilinear room

grabs everyone from snap-happy tourists to business lunchers and tutors them in the ways of sophisticated boozing. DJ's play jazz, soul and funk nightly; bridge views play 24/7.

PLAY

BANGARRA DANCE THEATRE *Dance*

☎ 9251 5333; www.bangarra.com.au; Pier 4 & 5, Hickson Rd, Walsh Bay, The Rocks; tickets $20-50; ♿ 🚼
Bangarra is hailed as Australia's finest Aboriginal dance company. Artistic director Stephen Page conjures a fusion of contemporary themes and indigenous traditions, blending Torres Strait Islander dance with Western technique. Often performing at the Sydney Opera House; bookings essential.

BONZA BIKE TOURS *Organised tour*

☎ 9331 1127; www.bonzabiketours .com; tours depart Portobello Caffé, Circular Quay East; tours $89/50; ⏱ 10.30am; 🚉 🚌 🚢 Circular Quay
These bonza bike boffins run daily 3½-hour 'Sydney Classic' bike tours – a great introduction to the harbour city, trundling past the Opera House, Hyde Park, Darling Harbour, Chinatown, Sydney Tower and the Royal Botanic Gardens. Ask about Manly and Sydney Highlights tours.

NEIGHBOURHOODS

THE ROCKS & CIRCULAR QUAY

Conquer the dizzying heights of the city's great bridge on the famous BridgeClimb

★ BRIDGECLIMB *Activity*

☎ 8274 7777; www.bridgeclimb.com;
5 Cumberland St, The Rocks; tours normal/
peak $169/249; 🚃 🚌 🚢 Circular Quay
Once only painters and daredevils
(including your author!) scaled
the Harbour Bridge heights, but
these days anyone can do it. Make
your way through the departure

lounge and extensive training session, don your headset, umbilical
cord and dandy grey jumpsuit
(Elvis would be so proud) and up
you go. The 3½-hour tours run
around the clock and there are
two climbs to choose from: the
famous BridgeClimb, and the new
Discovery Climb – less about the
view and 'personal achievement',

more about the nuts, bolts and internal workings.

🎬 DENDY OPERA QUAYS
Cinema

☎ 9247 3800; www.dendy.com.au; Shop 9, 2 Circular Quay East; tickets $15/12; 🕙 10.30am-9.45pm; 🚇 🚌 ⛴ Circular Quay; ♿

When the harbour glare and squawking seagulls get too much, duck into the dark folds of this plush cinema, screening first-run, independent world films, augmented by friendly attendants, a café and a bar. There's also the **Dendy Newtown** (Map p77, B5; ☎ 9550 5699; 261-3 King St).

🎬 NIGHT CAT TOURS
Organised tour

☎ 1300 551 608; www.nightcattours .com; tours depart Loftus St, Circular Quay; tours $69; 🕙 6.30-10pm Mon, Wed, Fri & Sat

Experience the good, the bad and the ugly of nocturnal Sydney with a small-group tour through the city, Balmain, McMahons Point, Woolloomooloo and Kings Cross. The tour includes two drinks and dinner – a salubrious 'Tiger' pie at Harry's Café de Wheels (p102).

🎬 SYDNEY DANCE COMPANY
Dance

☎ 9258 4818; www.sydneydance company.com; Pier 4 & 5, Hickson Rd,

Walsh Bay, The Rocks; tickets $29-69; 🚇 ⛴ Circular Quay 🚌 430-4; ♿

Under the direction of its inexhaustible choreographer Graeme Murphy, the SDC is Australia's No 1 contemporary dance company. For over 25 years Murphy has boogied-up the nation's cultural psyche with his wildly modern, sexy, sometimes shocking works, often performed at the Sydney Opera House. Cut the rug with a SDC dance lesson for $18!

🎬 SYDNEY FERRIES
Organised tour

☎ 9246 8300, 131 500; www.sydneyfer ries.nsw.gov.au; Wharf 4, Circular Quay; tours from $18/9; 🕙 morning 8am daily; afternoon 1pm Mon-Fri, 12.30pm Sat & Sun; evening 8pm Mon-Sat; 🚇 🚌 ⛴ Circular Quay; ♿

The city lights up for Sydney Ferries

If anyone's got the credentials to show you Sydney Harbour, it's Sydney Ferries. One- to 2½-hour morning, afternoon and evening harbour sights and lights cruises are available, chugging around on Sydney's cherished old ferries.

⚜ SYDNEY OPERA HOUSE
Theatre/live music/dance

☎ 9250 7777; www.sydneyoperahouse .com; Bennelong Pt, Circular Quay East; performances $25-220; ☺ box office 9am-8.30pm Mon-Sat, 2hr preshow Sun; 🚊 🚌 ⚓ Circular Quay; ♿

When it's not admiring itself in the mirror, the Opera House regularly hosts the **Australian Ballet** (☎ 1300 369 741; www.australianballet .com.au), **Australian Chamber Orchestra** (☎ 8274 3800; www.aco.com.au), Bangarra Dance Theatre (p59), **Bell Shakespeare** (☎ 8298 9016; www .bellshakespeare.com.au), **Musica Viva** (☎ 8694 6666; www.mva.org.au), **Opera Australia** (☎ 9699 1099; www.opera -australia.org.au), the Sydney Dance Company (p61), **Sydney Philharmonic Choirs** (☎ 9251 2024; www .sydneyphilharmonia.com.au), **Sydney Symphony** (☎ 8251 4600; www.sydneysymphony.com) and the Sydney Theatre Company (opposite). Phew…

⚜ SYDNEY THEATRE *Theatre*

☎ 9250 1999; www.sydneytheatre .org.au; 2 Hickson Rd, Walsh Bay, The Rocks; tickets $69-130; ☺ box office

9am-8.30pm Mon-Fri, from 11am Sat; 🚊 🚇 **Circular Quay** 🚌 430-4; ♿ Opening a few years ago with a name it seems odd no-one thought of before, the resplendent Sydney Theatre at the base of Observatory Hill puts 850 bums on seats for specialist drama and dance.

⭐ SYDNEY THEATRE COMPANY *Theatre*
☎ 9250 1777; www.sydneytheatre.com .au; Pier 4 & 5, Hickson Rd, Walsh Bay, The Rocks; tickets $20-130; ⏲ box office 9am-8.30pm, from 11am Sat; 🚊 🚇 **Circular Quay** 🚌 430-4; ♿ Working in tandem with the Sydney Theatre across the road, the STC is Sydney's premier theatre company. Major Australian actors (Barry Otto, Deborah Mailman) perform works by Alan Bennett, David Williamson and Shakespeare; smaller works play the Wharf, bigger shows play the Sydney Theatre and Opera House. Ask about $20 'Student Rush' tickets.

⭐ THE BASEMENT *Live music*
☎ 9251 2797; www.thebasement.com .au; 29 Reiby Pl, Circular Quay; tickets from $15; ⏲ noon-1.30am Mon-Thu, to 2.30am Fri, 7.30pm-3am Sat, 7pm-1am Sun; 🚊 🚌 🚇 **Circular Quay** Sydney's premier jazz venue presents big touring acts (Taj Mahal, Richard Buckner) and big

local talent (Vince Jones, Mia Dyson). A broad musical mandate also sees funk, blues and soul bands performing plus the odd spoken-word gig. Avoid the standing room-only bar; book a table by the stage.

⭐ THE ROCKS WALKING TOURS *Organised tour*
☎ 9247 6678; www.rockswalkingtours .com.au; 23 Playfair St, The Rocks; tours $20/11; ⏲ 10.30am, 12.30pm, & 2.30pm Mon-Fri, 11.30am & 2pm Sat & Sun; 🚊 🚌 🚇 **Circular Quay**; ♿ Ninety-minute tours of the historic Rocks that both entertain and exercise. These guys have been around since 1978, so they know The Rocks like the back of their hand(s).

⭐ WHALE WATCHING SYDNEY *Organised tour*
☎ 9583 1199; www.whalewatchingsyd ney.net; Eastern Pontoon, Circular Quay East; tours $80/72; ⏲ 9am & 1pm May-Nov; 🚊 🚌 🚇 **Circular Quay**; ♿ Humpback and Southern Right whales habitually shunt up and down the Sydney coastline, sometimes venturing into the harbour (p168). Whale Watching Sydney runs three-hour seasonal tours with a 98% sighting success rate! Tours also depart Pier 26 at Darling Harbour, 30 minutes prior to Circular Quay.

>CHINATOWN & DARLING HARBOUR

Sandwiched between the CBD and Darling Harbour, Sydney's Chinatown is a tight nest of restaurants, shops and aroma-filled alleyways around Dixon St. Food is what you're here for: top-notch Chinese, $5 food-court noodles and weekend yum cha. Shopping in Chinatown is fun too – whether you're on the scent of some incense, or tracking down a pseudo-Prada bag, the latest MP3 player or Hong Kong martial arts DVD, you'll find it here. Dipping into the hyper-commerce of Paddy's Markets is an essential Chinatown experience.

Darling Harbour (www.darlingharbour.com) is a rambling, purpose-built tourist park lining Cockle Bay on the city's western edge. Dotted between an architectural spoil of flyovers, fountains, sculptures and sailcloth are some great museums. The snazzy Cockle Bay Wharf and King Street Wharf precincts contain a dangerous array of cafés, bars and restaurants for when you're all museumed-out. Beneath the flocks of tourists and belligerent ibises, the harbour itself remains unflappably placid.

CHINATOWN & DARLING HARBOUR

◉ SEE
Australian National Maritime
  Museum 1 B2
Chinese Garden of
  Friendship 2 D5
Powerhouse Museum ... 3 C6
Sydney Aquarium 4 C3
Sydney Wildlife World ... 5 C2

◻ SHOP
Cyril's Fine Foods 6 E6
Good Living Growers'
  Market 7 B2

Paddy's Markets 8 D6
Ultimo Wine Centre 9 B6

🍴 EAT
BBQ King 10 D6
Blackbird 11 D3
Bungalow 8 .... 12 C1
Chinatown Noodle
  Restaurant 13 D7
Chinta Ria, Temple of
  Love 14 D3
Golden Century 15 D6
Xic Lo 16 D7
Zaaffran 17 C3

▼ DRINK
Cargo Bar 18 C2
Loft 19 C1

★ PLAY
Home 20 C4
James Craig 21 B1
Slip Inn 22 D2
Sydney by Sail 23 C3
Sydney Entertainment
  Centre 24 D6

Please see over for map

SEE

AUSTRALIAN NATIONAL MARITIME MUSEUM

☎ 9298 3777; www.anmm.gov.au; Darling Harbour; admission free, special exhibits from $10/6; ⏱ 9.30am-5pm; 🚊 Town Hall Ⓜ Harbourside 🚢 🏛 Pyrmont Bay; ♿

Beneath an Utzon-like roof, the Maritime Museum sails through Australia's inextricable relationship with the sea. Exhibitions range from Aboriginal canoes to surf culture and the navy. You can almost taste the salt.

CHINESE GARDEN OF FRIENDSHIP

☎ 9281 6863; www.chinesegarden .com.au; Darling Harbour; admission $6/3; ⏱ 9.30am-5pm; 🚊 Town Hall Ⓜ Garden Plaza 🚢 Exhibition Centre 🏛 Darling Harbour; ♿

Built according to the balanced principles of Yin and Yang, the Chinese Garden of Friendship is an oasis of tranquillity. Designed by architects from Guangzhou (Sydney's sister city) for Australia's bicentenary in 1988, the garden interweaves pavilions, waterfalls, lakes and paths – too

Learn about salt, sand and sails at the Australian National Maritime Museum

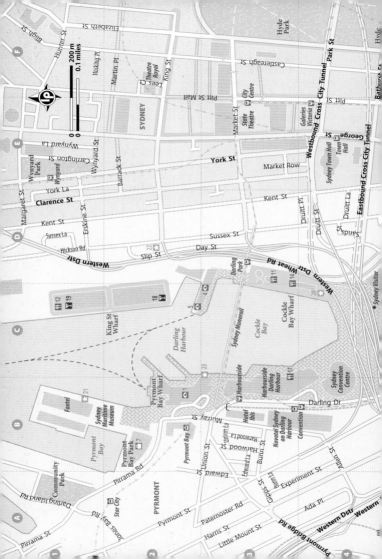

serene for words (so shut-up and be still).

☉ POWERHOUSE MUSEUM

☎ 9217 0100; www.powerhousemuseum.com; 500 Harris St, Ultimo; admission $10/6, special exhibits extra; 🕑 10am-5pm; Ⓜ Powerhouse Museum 🚊 Haymarket 🚌 501 from Town Hall; ♿

A short walk from Darling Harbour, Sydney's hippest and most progressive museum whirrs away inside the former power

station for Sydney's defunct tram network. High-voltage interactive demonstrations wow school groups with the low-down on how lightning strikes, magnets grab and engines growl.

☉ SYDNEY AQUARIUM

☎ 8251 7800; www.sydneyaquarium.com.au; Aquarium Pier, Darling Harbour; admission $28/19, AquariumPass incl admission & return ferry from Circular Quay $33/17; 🕑 9am-10pm, last admis-

Satisfy your inner geek at the Powerhouse Museum

SHARKY

Shark-o-phobia getting you down? A recent survey found that four species have been responsible for 94 Sydney shark attacks since 1791: Oceanic White Tip, Great White, Tiger and Bull sharks. Attacks peaked between 1920 and 1940, but since shark net installation began in 1937 there's only been one fatality (1963), and dorsal-fin sightings are rare enough to make the nightly news. Realistically, you're more likely to get hit by a bus, so get wet and enjoy yourself!

sion 9pm; 🚆 Town Hall Ⓜ Darling Park 🚌 Convention ⚓ Darling Harbour Aquarium; ♿

Aqua-fans enter through huge, kitsch metallic shark jaws into 160m of underwater tunnels, looking at 11,000 happy Australian sea creatures. Highlights include clown fish, humungous sharks in the Open Ocean section and the Great Barrier Reef exhibit's swoon-worthy Van Gogh coral colours. Residents of the Seal Sanctuary have lawless amounts of fun. Arrive early to beat the crowds (but less chatter makes it harder to ignore the piped indigestive whale noises).

🔵 SYDNEY WILDLIFE WORLD

☎ 9333 9288; www.sydneywildlife world.com.au; Aquarium Pier, Darling Harbour; admission $29/20, Wildlife World Pass incl return ferry from Circular Quay $34/18; ☽ 9am-10pm, last admission 9pm; 🚆 Town Hall Ⓜ Darling Park 🚌 Convention ⚓ Darling Harbour Aquarium; ♿

The newest of Darling Harbour's attractions costs a pretty penny, but it's a cut above the rest. And if

you don't have time to truck out to Taronga Zoo, this is your chance to check out some Aussie critters! Nine different habitats with 1km of walkways give you a sense of how wild life really is for koalas, wallabies, birds, butterflies and reptiles (among others). Feedings and demonstrations happen throughout the day. Ask about combined admission prices to Wildlife World and the Sydney Aquarium next door.

 SHOP

🔲 CYRIL'S FINE FOODS
Food & drink

☎ 9211 0994; 181 Hay St, Haymarket; ☽ 6am-5pm Mon-Fri, to 1pm Sat; 🚆 Central Ⓜ Powerhouse Museum 🚌 Capitol Square 🚌 George St buses

Cyril Vincent has opened his old-style deli at the crack of dawn for almost 50 years. Dawn doesn't seem to mind, and his loyal customers keep coming back for European smallgoods, chocolates, cheeses, coffee, mustards and variously pickled things at non-gourmet prices.

Paddy's Markets: an Aladdin's cave for bargain-hunters

GOOD LIVING GROWERS' MARKET *Market*

☎ 9282 3606; www.events.smh.com.au; Pyrmont Bay Park, Pyrmont; ⏱ 7-11am 1st Sat of each month; Ⓜ Harbourside
🚉 🚋 Pyrmont Bay

This picturesque, foodies' market not far from Darling Harbour showcases the best NSW regional produce. Peruse the 90 stalls packed with all sorts of delicacies from goat's cheese and sourdough bread to smoked tuna and wattleseed ice cream. Grab a coffee and reconstitute with an egg, bacon and chutney roll.

PADDY'S MARKETS *Market*

☎ 1300 361 589; www.paddysmarkets .com.au; cnr Hay & Thomas Sts, Haymarket; ⏱ 9am-5pm Thu-Sun; 🚉 Central Ⓜ Powerhouse Museum 🚋 Haymarket
🚌 George St buses

Paddy's is the Sydney equivalent of Istanbul's Grand Bazaar, but swap the incense, hookahs and carpets for mobile-phone covers, Eminem t-shirts and cheap sneakers. There's over 1000 stalls in this cavernous space – pick up a VB singlet for Uncle Bruce or wander the aisles in capitalist awe.

🍴 ULTIMO WINE CENTRE
Food & drink

☎ 9211 2380; www.ultimowinecentre
.com.au; 99 Jones St, Ultimo; 🕙 9am-
7pm Mon-Wed, to 8pm Thu & Fri, 10am-
8pm Sat, 11am-4pm Sun; 🚉 🚉 Central
🚌 501

Sydney's leading wine import specialist is just a cork's pop away from Darling Harbour, with wines divided regionally and special sections devoted to books and boozy accessories. Saturday-afternoon wine tasting sessions are timely.

🍴 EAT

🍴 BBQ KING *Cantonese* $$
☎ 9267 2433; fax 9267 2001; 18-20
Goulburn St, Chinatown; 🕙 11.30am-
2am; 🚉 Central 🚇 Garden Plaza
🚉 Capitol Square 🚌 George St buses;
V 👶

Low on ambience but big on flavour, the King serves up royal portions of roast duck, suckling pig and other Cantonese staples. You might need a Tsing Tao or three to stay sane amid the mildly obnoxious chaos. Take-away bald glazed ducks available next door; open late.

🍴 BLACKBIRD *Mod Oz* $$
☎ 9283 7385; www.blackbirdcafe.com
.au; Balcony, Cockle Bay Wharf, Darling
Harbour; 🕙 8am-late; 🚉 Town Hall

🚇 Darling Park 🚉 Convention 🏛 Darling Harbour Aquarium; ♿ V 👶

This place veritably thrums from the minute it opens its doors for breakfast. Funky young staff cruise the cool interior delivering hearty bowls of pasta, New York–style pizzas from the hot-stone oven and fat triangles of cake. Perfect to fuel up before or after a big night out.

🍴 BUNGALOW 8 *Seafood* $$
☎ 9299 4660; www.bungalow8sydney
.com; 8 The Promenade, King St Wharf,
Darling Harbour; 🕙 noon-late;
🚉 Wynyard 🚇 Darling Park
🚉 Harbourside 🏛 Darling Harbour
Aquarium; ♿

Retreat to the far end of King St Wharf if the mayhem of Darling Harbour starts to melt your mind. Slink into a low leather booth on the cool slate floor, watch the harbour lights and slurp a lemongrass laksa stacked high with fresh mussels. The Loft (p74) bar upstairs has cool cocktails afterwards.

🍴 CHINATOWN NOODLE RESTAURANT *Cantonese* $
☎ 9281 9051; Shop 7, Prince Centre,
8 Quay St, Chinatown (entry from Thomas
St); 🕙 11am-9pm; 🚉 Central 🚇 Powerhouse Museum 🚉 Capitol Square
🚌 George St buses; V 👶

It's sweaty, shoulder-to-shoulder eating beneath wreaths of plastic

NEIGHBOURHOODS

CHINATOWN & DARLING HARBOUR

CHINESE WHISPERS

Chinese people first came to Australia in 1840 when convict transportation ceased and labouring jobs became available. Thousands more arrived during the 1850s gold rush, but immigration stalled when the notorious 'White Australia' policy was enacted in 1861. In the 1870s Sydney's Chinese community gravitated to Dixon St, which rapidly became a commercial centre tainted with opium dens and gambling. It's here that perhaps China's greatest gift to Australia still thrills the crowds – fabulous Chinese food!

grapes in this busy noodle nook, where the stringy fare is made fresh daily. The combination dish looks like spaghetti bolognaise on steroids – masses of thick wheat noodles, pork, shredded cucumber and lashings of chilli and black vinegar.

🍴 CHINTA RIA, TEMPLE OF LOVE *Malaysian* $$

☎ 9264 3211; fax 9264 1411; L2, Cockle Bay Wharf, Darling Harbour; ⏰ noon-2.30pm Mon-Sat, 6-11pm daily; 🚆 Town Hall Ⓜ Darling Park 🚊 Convention 🚢 Darling Harbour Aquarium; 🚻 Ⓥ 👤

Swirling choreographically around an enormous concrete Buddha, Chinta Ria's temple-in-the-round offers zingy Malaysian hawker-

style food at reasonable prices. Go with a rabble of friends for Hokkien noodles, sambal prawns, seafood laksa, super-slippery fried *kuay teow* and flaki roti bread.

🍴 GOLDEN CENTURY
Cantonese seafood $$$

☎ 9212 3901; www.goldencentury .com.au; 393-9 Sussex St, Chinatown; ⏰ noon-4am; 🚆 Central Ⓜ Garden Plaza 🚊 Capitol Square 🚌 George St buses; 👤

The fish tank at this frenetic place forms a window-wall to the street, full of a whole lot o' nervous coral trout, king crab, barramundi, lobster and abalone. Splash out on the whole lobster cooked in ginger and shallots: tank-net-kitchen-you.

🍴 XIC LO *Vietnamese* $$

☎ 9280 1678; 215a Thomas St, Chinatown (entry from Ultimo Rd); ⏰ 11am-10.30pm Mon-Sat, to 10pm Sun; 🚆 Central Ⓜ Powerhouse Museum 🚊 Capitol Square 🚌 George St buses; Ⓥ 👤

Xic Lo's shiny, angular interior is a glossy departure from the *pho* houses of yore. The menu though is reassuringly familiar: fresh rice-paper rolls, vermicelli salads and piping-hot bowls of aromatic *pho* soup (slippery rice noodles, fragrant basil and beef) are the stars.

Feast on laksa, pho and rice-paper rolls in busting Chinatown

🍴 ZAAFFRAN *Indian* $$

☎ 9211 8900; www.zaaffran.com; L2, 345 Harbourside, Darling Harbour; 🕒 noon-3pm & 6-10pm; 🚇 Town Hall 🅼 🚇 Convention 🚋 Pyrmont Bay; ♿ Ⓥ

In a city with a gazillion cheap Indian joints, this is a standout. Authentic and innovative curries are served up with awesome views across Darling Harbour. Book a balcony seat and launch into the beef vindaloo.

DRINK

🍸 CARGO BAR *Bar*

☎ 9262 1777; www.cargobar.com .au; 52 The Promenade, King St Wharf, Darling Harbour; admission free; 🕒 11am-late; 🚇 Town Hall 🅼 Darling Park 🚋 Darling Harbour Aquarium; ♿

The definitive Darling Harbour bar lures beautiful boys, babes and backpackers who get wall-to-wall boozy after 11pm. It also has a cool kitchen: before the drinkers

NEIGHBOURHOODS

CHINATOWN & DARLING HARBOUR

descend, savour the harbour views and tasty pizzas and salads. DJs fire things up nightly; Sunday afternoon jazz mellows things down.

THE LOFT *Bar*
☎ 9299 4770; www.theloftsydney.com; 3 Lime St, Darling Harbour; admission free; 🕑 4pm–1am Mon-Wed, to 3am Thu, noon–3am Fri & Sat, noon–1am Sun; 🚉 Wynyard Ⓜ Darling Park 🚢 Harbourside 🚢 Darling Harbour Aquarium
The Loft is far from lofty – it's more like an open-plan office space – but the walls fold back and disappear, sweeping your eye out across Darling Harbour and beyond. Interior design is 'Moroccan Chic'; service is snappy. Book for high tea at 1pm on weekends.

⭐ PLAY
⭐ HOME *Club*
☎ 9266 0600; www.homesydney.com; Cockle Bay Wharf, Darling Harbour; admission $25; 🕑 11pm–6am Fri, 9pm–6am Sat; 🚉 Town Hall Ⓜ Darling Park 🚢 Darling Harbour Aquarium;
Welcome to the pleasure dome: a three-level, 2000-capacity timber and glass 'prow' that's home to a huge dance floor, countless bars, outdoor balconies and sonics that make other clubs sound like transistor radios. Catch top-name

international DJs spinning a homey house smorgasbord, plus live bands amping it up.

⭐ JAMES CRAIG
Organised tour
☎ 9298 3888; www.sydneyheritage fleet.com.au; Wharf 7, Pyrmont; tickets $195/160; 🕑 10.30am–5pm every 2nd weekend Sep–May, 9.30am–4pm Jun–Aug; Ⓜ Harbourside 🚢 Pyrmont Bay; 🚢
The James Craig is a hulking, black, three-masted iron barque built in Sunderland, England in 1874. Abandoned in Tasmania in the '30s, she was floated to Sydney and restored in the '70s. Square-rigged sails billow as you sail out through the Heads on the open-ocean swell. Price includes lunch, morning/afternoon teas and a sea shanty or three.

⭐ SLIP INN *Club*
☎ 8297 7000; www.merivale.com; 111 Sussex St; admission free–$15; 🕑 noon–4am Thu & Fri, 6pm–4am Sat; 🚉 Wynyard Ⓜ Darling Park 🚢 Darling Harbour Aquarium; 🚢
Slip in to this warren of moody rooms on the edge of Darling Harbour and bump hips with the cool kids. Can you believe Crown Prince Frederik of Denmark met his Tasmanian missus here? Resident and international selectors serve up old-school funk, latin,

CHINATOWN & DARLING HARBOUR

breaks, tech and house. Refuel on pizza and Thai.

⭐ **SYDNEY BY SAIL** *Activity*
☎ 9280 1110; www.sydneybysail.com.au; Festival Pontoon, National Maritime Museum, Darling Harbour; tour $130, course $425; 🕙 9am-5pm; 🚊 Town Hall Ⓜ Harbourside 🚋 🛳 Pyrmont Bay
Driving around driving you mad? Sydney by Sail runs a daily sailing tour and a comprehensive introductory weekend sailing course. Knots, fathoms, hulls, bilges, spinnakers, tacking and gibing – 12 hours on the water will ensure you're shipshape.

⭐ **SYDNEY ENTERTAINMENT CENTRE** *Live music*
☎ 9320 4200; www.sydentcent.com.au; 35 Harbour St, Haymarket; 🕙 box office 9am-5pm Mon-Fri; 🚊 Central Ⓜ Powerhouse Museum 🚋 Haymarket; ♿ 🚻
Sydney's largest indoor venue holds 12,000 howling rock fans, recent acts including Pink, Beyoncé, John Mayer and (the rather haggard looking) INXS. Its padded purple seats also fill with kids going nuts for the Wiggles and Disney On Ice, and it's home court for the Sydney Kings basketball team (p158).

>INNER WEST

Paddington and the Eastern Beaches define Sydney at face value, but the Inner West digs deeper and comes up with something resembling a soul. This is where anyone with any sense of quirkiness hangs out – students, Goths, urban hippies, junkies, poets, painters, writers and sexual subculturists. Streets and shop windows have a decidedly less polished appearance around here – more graffiti, less Gucci.

Glebe focuses on Glebe Point Rd, a long, undulating strip of cafés, bookshops and eateries. The mood here is chilled-out, but the Saturday market (p78) injects some vigour – stock up on retro duds, jewellery, sunglasses and vinyl, and save space for a funky vego lunch. Newtown is much more hustle-and-bustle, the sinuous snake of King St is crammed tightly with restaurants, pubs, yoga studios and second-hand CD shops. This is also the spiritual home of Sydney's lesbian community. Further west are low-key Camperdown, rockin' Annandale, and leafy, affluent Balmain.

INNER WEST

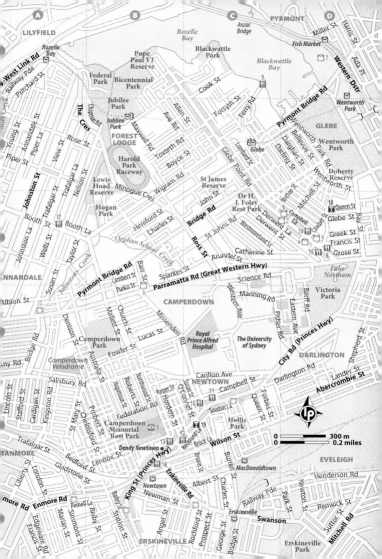

SEE

CAMPERDOWN CEMETERY

☎ 9557 2043; 187 Church St, Newtown; admission free; ☼ 6am-7pm; ⓡ Newtown 🚌 422-3, 426, 428; ♿

Take a self-guided tour beyond the monstrous 1848 fig tree into this dark, eerily unkempt cemetery. Many famous early Australians were buried here between 1849 and 1942, including Eliza Donnithorne, the inspiration for Miss Havisham in Dickens' *Great Expectations*.

SHOP

ARCHITECTURAL HERITAGE
Antiques

☎ 9660 0100; www.architecturalheritage.com.au; 62 Glebe Point Rd, Glebe; ☼ 10am-6pm; 🚌 431-4

Take a trip into this strange world of suspended history and architectural salvage. To the tune of piped Gatsby swing, explore two jam-packed levels of babbling fountains, stained-glass windows, wrought-iron balustrades, marble hearths, bronze sculptures, urns, staircases and figureheads from places entirely elsewhere and more mysterious.

DEUS EX MACHINA
Fashion

☎ 9519 3983; www.deusexmachina.com.au; 98-104 Parramatta Rd, Camperdown; ☼ 10am-6pm Mon-Fri, to 4pm Sat; 🚌 438, L38, 413, 440

Literally: 'God out of a machine', this is the perfect example of how big cities allow weird specialisations to flourish. Crammed with classic and custom-made motorcycles, this is 'post-modern motorcyclism' at its best – part workshop, part café, part offbeat boutique.

GLEBE MARKET *Market*

☎ 4237 7499; Glebe Public School, cnr Glebe Point Rd & Derby Pl, Glebe; ☼ 9am-4pm Sat; 🚌 431-4

If you missed Woodstock, you'll find its dreadlocked, shoeless legacy here. Inner-city hippies

---

WORTH THE TRIP

Milling around the shady grounds of St Andrews Congregational, **Balmain Market** (☎ 0418 765 736; cnr Darling St & Curtis Rd, Balmain; ☼ 8.30am-4pm Sat; 🚢 Balmain East 🚌 432-4, 441-2, 445) features stalls selling arts, crafts, books, clothing, jewellery, plants and fruit and veg, all jumbled together like socks in a drawer. The church itself is open if you want a Middle Eastern snack or need to consult St Andy about a prospective purchase.

beat a hazy course to this crowded Saturday market. Once massaged, fuelled on lentil burgers and swathed in funky retro gear, they retreat to the lawns, pass the peace pipe and chill-out to an African drum soundtrack.

📷 **GLEEBOOKS** *Bookshop*
☎ 9660 2333; www.gleebooks.com.au; 49 Glebe Point Rd, Glebe; 🕙 9am-9pm; 🚌 431-4
Gleebooks – a ramshackle two-storey terrace house – is generally regarded as Sydney's best

Get your motor runnin' at Deus Ex Machina

Thumb through the volumes at Sydney's much-loved Gleebooks

bookshop. The aisles are packed with politics, arts and general fiction and staff know their stuff backwards. Its annual literary programme attracts big-name local (Winton, Leunig etc) and international writers. Children's and second-hand books are at the second branch at 191 Glebe Point Rd.

🏠 SYDNEY FISH MARKET
Food & drink

☎ 9004 1122; www.sydneyfishmarket .com.au; Bank St, Pyrmont; ⏱ 7am-4pm; 🚊 Fish Market 🚌 501, 443

This piscatorial precinct on Blackwattle Bay has restaurants, a deli, wine centre, oyster bar, florist, seafood school, early morning auctions and behind-the-scenes auction tours ($20; 6.55am Monday and Thursday). Chefs, locals and overfed seagulls haggle over mud crabs, Balmain bugs, lobsters and slabs of salmon.

EAT

BADDE MANORS *Café* $

☎ 9660 3797; www.baddemanorscafe.com; 37 Glebe Point Rd, Glebe; ⏱ 8am-midnight Mon-Thu, to 1am Fri & Sat, 9am-midnight Sun; 🚌 431-4; V ♿

The feeling's eclectically old-world, but Badde Manors is a new-age kinda joint. It can get hectic here, but service remains cool and composed – no sign of the alleged bad manners. Dogs sleep blissfully outside, dreaming of the Portuguese custard tarts and rhubarb crumble behind the glass.

BOATHOUSE ON BLACKWATTLE BAY
Seafood $$$

☎ 9518 9011; www.boathouse.net.au; end of Ferry Rd, Glebe; ⏱ noon-3pm & 6-10pm Tue-Sun; 🚇 Glebe 🚌 431-4

The best restaurant in Glebe, and one of the best seafood restaurants in Sydney. Offerings range from oysters so fresh you'd think you shucked them yourself, to a snapper pie that'll go straight to the top of your favourite dish list. Anzac Bridge views; reservations essential.

CAMPOS *Café* $

☎ 9516 3361; www.camposcoffee.com; 193 Missenden Rd, Newtown; ⏱ 7am-4pm Mon-Fri, 8am-5pm Sat; 🚇 Newtown 🚌 422-3, 426, 428; ♿

Trying to squeeze into crowded Campos, king of Sydney's bean-scene, can be a challenge. Caffeine fiends come from miles around – hat-wearing students, broadsheet literati, window-seat daydreamers and doctors on a break from the hospital – all gagging for a shot of 'Campos Superior' blend. The closest competition is in northern Italy.

GREEN GOURMET
Vegetarian $

☎ 9519 5330; www.greengourmet.com.au; 115 King St, Newtown; ⏱ noon-3pm & 6-10pm; 🚇 Newtown 🚌 422-3, 426, 428; V

Green Gourmet is a self-serve, pay-per-kilo, kind-to-animals eatery, plating up Chinese-Malaysian vegetarian at affordable prices. On weekends, grab a few morsels of cruelty-free yum cha and wash it down with one of the excellent teas on offer. Alcohol-free too.

Ben D'Emden
Barista at Campos, Newtown (p81)

Been working here long? Four and a half years. All the baristas aspire to work here! **What does it take to be a top Sydney barista?** A lot of concentration. You have to be obsessed with coffee – get involved with it – and you've got to be passionate when you talk to people. You need to pay attention to detail – to be able to look at a cup and go, 'That's no good, let's do it again'. Having a good roaster helps too. **Do Sydneysiders appreciate good coffee?** In the last five years, people have started demanding better coffee. Nowadays we're catering to new, savvy coffee drinkers. **Most popular brew?** Flat whites rule the roost, but lately we've been making more espresso – shorter drinks, more European-style. **Best thing about working here?** Apart from the coffee, the diversity of Newtown is great – young people, students, gays, straights… It's a cool place.

Dark City
$9.50/250g

Campos Superior
Blend
$8.50/250g

Bourbon Street
Gourmet
$9.00/250g

WORTH THE TRIP

The culinary highlight of Leichhardt, Sydney's Italian district just west of Annandale, is **Grappa** (☎ 9560 6090; www.grappa.com.au; Shop 1, 267-77 Norton St, Leichhardt; ⏰ 6-10pm Mon, noon-3pm & 6-10pm Tue-Fri, 6-11pm Sat, noon-3pm & 6-9.30pm Sun; 🚌 413, 435-8, 440; ♿). An open kitchen, snazzy bar and cream-leather seats provide the setting for rich, succulent dishes (like baked snapper in rock-salt crust) and bounteous wood-fired pizzas. If it's warm, sit outside on the terrace, sip Chianti and think of Tuscany. *Ahhh*, Tuscany…

🍴 KILIMANJARO *African* $$
☎ 9557 4565; fax 9565 1869; 280 King St, Newtown; ⏰ 1-3pm Wed-Sun, 6-10pm Mon-Fri, to 11pm Sat & Sun; 🚆 Newtown 🚌 422-3, 426, 428; V

The cosy tables, carved-wooden bowls, saffron aromas and cheery atmosphere will raise your appetite high above the Serengeti. Authentic East African dishes like the *yassa* (chicken on the bone marinated in spicy tomato sauce) are utterly filling. Check out the crafty Africa mural on the alleyway wall!

🍴 OLD FISH SHOP CAFÉ
Café $
☎ 9519 4295; fax 9565 1532; 239a King St, Newtown; ⏰ 6am-7pm; 🚆 Newtown 🚌 422-3, 426, 428; ♿ V

In a converted fish shop (no prizes for figuring that out), this is Newtown's tattooed, dreadlocked, caffeine-hungry hub. Friendly pierced staff will fix you a double shot as you put your feet up on the cushions in the window and watch the freak-show on the street.

🍴 OSTERIA DEI POETI
Italian $$
☎ 9571 8955; 73 Glebe Point Rd, Glebe; ⏰ noon-2.30pm Fri & Sat, 6-10pm Mon-Thu, to 10.30pm Fri & Sat; 🚌 431-4; ♿ V

Fostering 'benign benevolence' through stomach satisfaction, the talkative 'Tavern of Poets' serves unpretentious, home-style Italian that's poetic enough to be beyond most domestic kitchens. If the occasional poetry readings are overly florid, head for the deck outside.

🍴 SPANISH TAPAS
Spanish $$
☎ 9571 9005; fax 9518 6371; 26 Glebe Point Rd, Glebe; ⏰ noon-3pm Thu-Sat, 6-11pm daily; 🚌 431-4; V ♿

This is a good-time restaurant: shared tapas plates, spirited music, raucous diners and waiters who say, 'Yezz, we jave a table forl yo'. Cheap jugs of sangria will dissolve any party resistance and fire you up for flamenco dancing displays.

V

Sample seafood delights at the Boathouse on Blackwattle Bay (p81)

🍴 THAI POTHONG *Thai* $$

☎ 9550 6277; www.thaipothong.com.au; 294 King St, Newtown; ⏱ noon-3pm Tue-Sun, 6-10pm Sun-Thu, 6-11pm Fri & Sat; 🚆 Newtown 🚌 422-3, 426, 428; Ⓥ ♿

This place has won a bowlful of 'Best Thai Restaurant in Sydney' awards. The menu is predictable and the usual rabble of golden Buddhas festoons the walls, but the mood is oddly romantic. Pull up a window seat and watch the Newtowners pass onwards to oblivion.

🍴 ZENITH *Italian* $$

☎ 9660 6600; zenithonbooth@hotmail.com; 37 Booth St, Annandale; ⏱ 9am-1pm Sat & Sun, 6-10pm Tue-Sat; 🚆 Jubilee Park 🚌 470; Ⓥ ♿

Started by Mario Percuoco, son of Armando of Buon Ricordo fame (p118), Zenith delivers *bellissimo* thin-crust pizzas and contemporary Italian dishes in an improbably gorgeous two-storey Victorian corner terrace, complete with overhanging balcony. Weekend breakfasts are mayhem.

DRINK

🍸 FRIEND IN HAND HOTEL
Pub

☎ 9660 2326; www.friendinhand.com.au; 58 Cowper St, Glebe; admission free; ⏱ 10am-late; 🚌 431-4; ♿

This place has changed the rules of what's supposed to happen

---

WORTH THE TRIP

The Harbour Bridge views from the long balcony at Balmain's **London Hotel** (☎ 9555 1377; www.thelondonhotel.com.au; 234 Darling St, Balmain; admission free; ⏱ 11am-midnight Mon-Sat, noon-10pm Sun; 🚢 Balmain East 🚌 432-4, 441-2, 445) are quintessentially Sydney (about as far from London as you can get). There's a great range of Oz beers on tap, plus a few quality Euro interlopers (Heineken, Hoegaarden et al), jovial punters and nonstop rugby on the telly.

---

in an Australian pub. Sure, you can drink all the beer you want, but don't be surprised when the eating competitions, water-pistol fights, crab racing, stand-up comedians, cheesy Joel/John piano men and hula-hoop spin-offs cut into your drinking time.

🍸 NEWTOWN HOTEL *Pub*

☎ 9517 1728; www.newtownhotel.com; 174 King St, Newtown; admission free; ⏱ 11am-midnight Mon-Fri, 10am-midnight Sat, 10am-10pm Sun; 🚆 Newtown 🚌 422-3, 426, 428; ♿

The Newtown does a heady G&L trade with folk who just want to go to the local boozer and have a few laughs. Musical stimulation is provided by the sensational sequined drag acts like Portia Turbo and Pru Crimson.

PLAY

ANNANDALE HOTEL
Live music

☎ 9550 1078; www.annandalehotel
.com; cnr Parramatta Rd & Nelson
St, Annandale; admission free-$30;
⏱ 11am-midnight Tue-Sat, to 10pm
Sun, to 11pm Mon; 🚆 Stanmore 🚌 413,
435-8, 440, 461; ♿

The Annandale survived Sydney's
live-music morgue in the '90s and
now spearheads Sydney's rock
revival, coughing up nightly alt-
rock, metal, punk and electronica.
Afroed punters traverse the sticky
carpet between sets by Thirsty
Merc, the Dandy Warhols and
Jet. 'F*£k this, I'm going to the
Annandale!'.

EMPIRE HOTEL *Live music*

☎ 9557 1701; www.empirelive.com
.au; cnr Parramatta Rd & Johnston
St, Annandale; admission free-$20;
⏱ 9am-3pm Mon-Sat, 10am-midnight
Sun; 🚆 Stanmore 🚌 413, 435-8, 440,
461; ♿

The Empire's well-managed
300-capacity bar gets down 'n'
dirty with some of Sydney's best
blues and roots. Local bands with
loyal followings play free gigs;
listen out for international artists
and regular metal, ska, rockabilly,
country-and-western and swing
dancing nights!

WORTH THE TRIP

The well-restored late-Victorian **Dawn
Fraser Baths** (☎ 9555 903; www.lmc
.nsw.gov.au/dawn-fraser-baths.html;
Elkington Park, Glassop St, Balmain; admission $3.50/2; ⏱ 7.15am-6.15pm
Oct, Nov, Mar & Apr, 6.45am-7pm Dec-
Feb; 🚌 432-4, 441-2, 445) are worth
a look. Built in 1884, the enclosure
protects swimmers from underwater
undesirables. Australia's all-conquering
1956–64 Olympian Dawn Fraser spent
far too long swimming laps here.

ENMORE THEATRE
Live music

☎ 9550 3666; www.enmoretheatre
.com.au; 130 Enmore Rd, Newtown;
tickets $20-60; ⏱ box office 9am-6pm
Mon-Fri, 10am-4pm Sat; 🚆 Newtown
🚌 422-3, 426, 428; ♿ 🚼

Originally a vaudeville playhouse,
the elegantly wasted Enmore
now hosts acts like Queens of the
Stone Age, Wilco and PJ Harvey,
plus theatre and comedy. The
1600-capacity theatre feels like
an old-time movie hall, with café,
wooden floors, lounge areas and
balconies.

IMPERIAL HOTEL *Club/pub*

☎ 9519 9899; www.theimperialhotel
.com.au; 35 Erskineville Rd, Erskineville;
admission free; ⏱ 3pm-midnight, to
2.30am Thu, to 6am Fri & Sat; 🚆 Erskineville, Newtown 🚌 422-3, 426, 428

The Art Deco Imperial's drag shows inspired *Priscilla, Queen of the Desert* (the opening scene was filmed here). Any drag queen worth her sheen has played the Cabaret Room, while the Cellar Bar, Public Bar and Priscilla Lounge heave with chesty pool boys and raging house.

⭐ SANDRINGHAM HOTEL
Live music

☎ 9557 1254; fax 9517 9325; 387 King St, Newtown; admission free-$15; 🕑 11am-midnight Mon-Sat, to 10pm Sun; 🚇 Newtown; 🚌 422-3, 426, 428

We were nervous the Sando's renovations would spell the end of live music here, but thankfully, you can still get rocked from Tuesday to Sunday for not much money.

Acoustic acts upstairs; Goth-metal on Sunday night.

⭐ VANGUARD *Live music*

☎ 9557 7992; www.thevanguard.com.au; 42 King St, Newtown; dinner & show from $36, general admission $10-40; 🕑 dinner from 7pm, music from 8pm; 🚇 Newtown; 🚌 422-3, 426, 428

Freethinking, intellectual, artistic, musical – the qualities to which the Vanguard aspires. The intimate, time-travelling 1920s-themed band room satisfies these criteria; occasional Russell Crowe gigs, however, do not. Ed Kuepper and Rebecca Barnard shows are redemptive. Most seats are reserved for dinner-and-show diners.

>SURRY HILLS

Jammed between Darlinghurst and the city, Surry Hills is home to a raffish, noir mishmash of inner-city groovers and yuppies, many of whom rarely venture beyond their favourite (and admittedly excellent) local pubs and eateries. Fed and watered, they drift back to their slick warehouse apartments, remnants of the rag trade and print industry upon which Surry Hills built its reputation. But don't expect much gritty blue-collar struggle around here – life for 'Surry Hillbillies' these days is decadent, comfortable and sophisticated.

Most of the Surry Hills action centres on Crown St and Bourke St, heading south from the city – both streets have clusters of excellent restaurants, cafés and pubs. Surry Hills also sustains a collection of cutting-edge and crafty galleries (including the converted studio of legendary Surry Hills local Brett Whiteley), actively engaging in artsy sabre-rattling with the snootier rival galleries in Paddington, and the hip new galleries along Danks St in Waterloo.

SURRY HILLS

◉ SEE

🛍 SHOP

🍴 EAT

🍸 DRINK

★ PLAY

SEE

BRETT WHITELEY STUDIO

☎ 9225 1881; www.brettwhiteley.org;
2 Raper St; admission $7/5; ⏱ 10am-
4pm Sat & Sun; 🚆 🚇 Central 🚌 301-3,
343, 372

Whiteley was rock 'n' roll artistry –
he lived fast and without restraint,
and when he let fly on the canvas,
everybody went '*Ooohh!*' His studio
has been preserved as a gallery for
some of his best work. Get in early
for weekend discussions, performances, readings and workshops.

OBJECT GALLERY

☎ 9361 4555; www.object.com.au; 415
Bourke St; admission free; ⏱ 11am-6pm

Brett Whiteley's most intriguing works are preserved in this studio-turned-gallery

Tue-Sun; 🚈 Central 🚌 371, 373, 377, 380, 396; ♿

Inside the former St Margaret's Hospital chapel (a 1958 modernist classic by architect Ken Woolley), nonprofit Object presents innovative exhibitions of new craft and design from Australia and overseas. Furniture, fashion, textiles and glass festoon three levels.

🎨 RAY HUGHES GALLERY
☎ 9698 3200; www.rayhughesgallery.com; 270 Devonshire St; admission free; 🕙 10am-6pm Tue-Sat; 🚈 🚈 Central 🚌 301

Beyond the corrugated-iron cows and enormous wooden fish, old-time art dealer Ray Hughes wheels and deals. The Australian and contemporary Chinese and African art he flogs is some of Sydney's classiest. Even if you don't buy a cow, his bohemian warehouse is worth a look.

🛍 SHOP
🏠 SPENCE & LYDA *Homewares*
☎ 9292 6747; www.spenceandlyda.com.au; 16 Foster St; 🕙 10am-4pm Mon-Sat; 🚈 🚈 Central M World Square 🚌 308-10, 343

Solid but far from rustic, bright but never garish, the Italian and US kitchenware, fabrics, furnishings, lamps, linen, glassware and rugs in this snazzy showroom will make even the most determined travellers want to go home and feather the nest. Don't be deterred by the stern, deskbound staff – they're actually very bored and are delighted to help.

🏠 SYDNEY ANTIQUE CENTRE
Antiques
☎ 9361 3244; www.sydantcent.com.au; 531 South Dowling St; 🕙 10am-6pm; 🚌 339, 340, 373-4, 390

Sydney's oldest antique shop, the capacious Sydney Antique Centre has over 60 dealers specialising in porcelain, silver, glass, collectables and furniture. Items range from sports memorabilia to antique grandfather clocks and Art Deco jewellery. Pick up a 19th-century alabaster mannequin and drag it through the café and bookshop.

🍴 EAT
🍴 BILLY KWONG *Chinese* $$
☎ 9332 3300; fax 9332 4109; 3/355 Crown St; 🕙 6-10pm Mon-Sat, to 9pm Sun; 🚈 🚈 Central 🚌 301-3, 391; ♿

Chef Kylie Kwong's novel take on Chinese cuisine soon explains why this hip eating house is always so busy. You can't go wrong with staples like spicy, diced, fried green beans with hoisin and garlic, or a generous serve of Kylie's signature dish, the crispy-skin duck with plum sauce.

NEIGHBOURHOODS

SURRY HILLS

🍴 BIRD COW FISH
Bistro/deli $$
☎ 9380 4090; www.birdcowfish.com.au;
500 Crown St; 🕐 8am-11pm Mon-Sat, to
4pm Sun; 🚍 301-3, 391; 🚻
As the name suggests, there's
plenty of creatively prepared flesh
on BCF's menu, but locals and
cross-town venturers are here as
much for the munificent *fromage* as
the meat. Forty boutique Oz and in-
ternational cheeses generate quite
a whiff in the corner deli. Oh, and
the espresso's as good as it gets!

🍴 BOOK KITCHEN *Café* $$
☎ 9310 1003; www.thebookkitchen
.com.au; 255 Devonshire St; 🕐 8am-
4pm daily, 6.30-10.30pm Thu-Sat;
🚍 301-3, 391; 🔲 🚻
Sunny pavement tables, attentive
service, walls of foody books, a
braised Wagyu beef and mustard
sandwich and a Book Kitchen
Bloody Mary – sometimes life
just comes together perfectly
doesn't it?

🍴 BOURKE ST BAKERY *Café* $
☎ 9699 1011; 633 Bourke St; 🕐 7am-
7pm Tue-Fri, 8am-5pm Sat & Sun;
🚍 301-3, 391; 🚻 🔲 🚻
It hasn't been around that long,
but the Bourke St Bakery has
quickly become an essential
Surry Hills experience, offering
up a mean selection of pastries,
cakes, croissants, tarts, quiches

and organic breads, all baked with
that rare combo of deliciousness,
dedication and delight. If you're
hung-over, the coffee will right
your rudder.

🍴 LONGRAIN *Thai* $$$
☎ 9280 2888; www.longrain.com.au;
85 Commonwealth St; 🕐 noon-2.30pm
Mon-Fri, 6-11pm Mon-Sat, bar 5.30pm-
midnight Mon-Sat; 🔲 🔲 Central
Ⓜ World Square 🚍 308-10, 343;
🚻 🔲
Longrain makes serving dozens of
louche diners look easy. Inside a
century-old, wedge-shaped print-
ing-press building, urbanites slurp
down delicacies like red venison
and snakebean curry or caramel-
ised pork hock with five spices and
chilli vinegar. Sip a caipiroska at
the bar afterwards.

🍴 MARQUE *French* $$$
☎ 9332 2225; www.marquerestaurant
.com.au; 355 Crown St; 🕐 6.30-10pm Mon-
Sat; 🔲 🔲 Central 🚍 301-3, 391; 🚻
Marque's crisp, immaculate décor
provides a level-headed platform
for adventurous cooking. It's one
of those places where culinary
experimentation at first seems
ridiculous, but you walk away
smiling. Try the milk-fed veal
loin with Meyer lemon, liquorice,
pumpkin and coffee.

Catherine Mundy,
Researcher for jtv, ABC Television

What do you love about Surry Hills? The nice old guy at the corner shop who nearly always rounds down and gives me 10 or 20 cents off. **Favourite Surry Hills eatery?** The little Japanese pancake stall at the Surry Hills Markets (www.surryhillsneighbourhoodcentre.org.au). **Best place for a drink?** The Hotel Hollywood (p94) and the Cricketers Arms Hotel (p94), my two favourite pubs. **How about a kick-arse coffee?** The Bourke St Bakery (opposite) is great. It's a tiny nook with a perpetual line of folk queuing into the street for croissants, rhubarb danishes, pistachio *crème brûlée*… But I only go there for the coffee. Really. **Is the Sydney live music scene rockin', or is it just clubs, clubs, clubs?** The indie music scene is pretty big here, but there's still much to be said for a trashy club bender in The Cross.

🍴 MOHR FISH *Seafood* $$

☎ 9318 1326; www.mohrandmohr.com.au; 202 Devonshire St; ⏲ noon-3pm Mon-Fri, 6-10pm daily; 🚇 🚉 Central 🚌 301-3, 391

Teutonic iron chef Hans Mohr started this fishy takeaway decades ago, and just when we thought he'd reached his punny pinnacle, he opened Mohr & Morh restaurant next door. Both serve sensational seafood with Euro stylings; the restaurant is more structured but still casual.

🍴 PIZZA E BIRRA *Italian* $$

☎ 9332 2510; 1/500 Crown St; ⏲ 6-11pm Mon-Wed, noon-11pm Thu-Sun; 🚌 301-3, 391; ♿ Ⓥ 👶

Bentwood chairs clatter across the polished concrete floor; friends laugh, clink glasses and unwind; waiters spin, smile and style – Pizza e Birra is the perfect neighbourhood bistro, with enough style to be cool, and enough familiarity to be comfortable. Try the classic Napoletana pizza: tomato, mozzarella, olives and anchovies, washed down with a cold Peroni.

🍴 TABOU *French* $$$

☎ 9319 5682; fax 9319 5805; 527 Crown St; ⏲ 6.30pm-late daily, noon-2.30pm Mon-Fri; 🚌 301-3, 391

Not out of place on Boulevard Saint-Michel, Tabou's stained-glass shopfront and lilting accordion music are French to the core. Brasserie dishes, including perennial faves like duck confit, *lapin de la moutard* and steak tartare, paint the scene Gallic. *Vive la France*!

🍸 DRINK

🍸 CRICKETERS ARMS HOTEL *Pub*

☎ 9331 3301; www.cricketers.com.au; 106 Fitzroy St; admission free; ⏲ noon-midnight Mon-Sat, to 10pm Sun; 🚇 🚉 Central 🚌 374

The polysexual cricketers, with its cruisy, cosy vibe, is a favourite haunt of arts students, locals, gays and turntable fans. It's ace for a beer anytime, and there's tapas on tap and open fires for those rare times Sydney actually gets cold.

🍸 HOTEL HOLLYWOOD *Pub*

☎ 9281 2765; www.hotelhollywood.com.au; 2 Foster St; admission free; ⏲ 11am-midnight Mon-Wed, to 3am Thu-Sat; 🚇 🚉 Central Ⓜ World Square 🚌 308-10, 343

An inner-city, prow-shaped, Art Deco gem, the Hollywood hasn't felt the need to buff itself up to a superficial sheen. A mixed (dare we say, bohemian) crowd of Surry Hillbillies gets down to serious beer business. Live jazz Monday to Thursday from 8pm.

OUT ON THE TILES

Most of Sydney's older pubs are clad in glazed tiles, often with beautifully coloured Art Nouveau designs. Why? Prior to drinking law reform in the mid-1950s, pubs shut their doors at 6pm, before which after-work drinkers would storm in and chug down as many beers as quickly as possible – the '6 o'clock swill'. This, plus the sudden requirement of walking, caused frequent regurgitations, the nearest wall becoming a prop for the trembling vomiter. Publicans discovered pretty quickly that glazed tiles are easy to hose down.

☗ MARS LOUNGE *Bar*

☎ 9267 6440; www.marslounge.com
.au; 16 Wentworth Ave; admission free;
☼ 5pm-midnight Tue, Wed & Sun, to
3am Thu-Sat; ☒ Museum Ⓜ World
Square ☒ 308-10, 343

Red leather booths; disco-ball reflections catching in the corner of your eye – Mars is *sooo* money. Sip a cocktail and try to stay focussed as you watch the bar staff in action, most of whom seem to be auditioning for a gig in a Justin Timberlake video.

PLAY

☗ COMPANY B *Theatre*

☎ 9699 3444; www.belvoir.com.au; Belvoir Street Theatre, 25 Belvoir St; tickets from $48/30; ☼ box office 9.30am-6pm Mon & Tue, to 7.30pm Wed-Sat, 2.30-7.30pm Sun; ☒ ☒ Central; ♿

Artistic director Neil Armfield is the darling of the Sydney theatre world. Cinema stars like Geoffrey Rush clamour to perform his interpretations of modern masters like David Hare in the recently refurbished Belvoir St Theatre. Bookings advised.

☗ GAELIC CLUB *Live music*

☎ 9211 1687; www.thegaelicclub
.com.au; 64 Devonshire St; tickets $10-30; ☒ ☒ Central ☒ Railway Sq buses

Rock into the Gaelic Club and get your earwax blasted out courtesy of iconic internationals like Helmet and The Strokes, or home-grown sonic assailants like Wolfmother, Silverchair and You Am I. It's a midsize, split-level, multipurpose affair – much beer and moshing.

☗ HOPETOUN HOTEL
Live music

☎ 9361 5257; fax 9331 8145; 416 Bourke St; admission free-$15;
☼ noon-midnight Mon-Sat, to 10pm Sun; ☒ ☒ Central ☒ 374

Once the uncontested crucible for new Sydney rock bands, the diminutive 'Hoey' is still a launch pad for garage bands on the boil. On Sunday afternoon it transforms into a low-key space with DJs and night-crawlers knocking the froth off a few cold ones before they hit the sack.

>KINGS CROSS, DARLINGHURST & AROUND

Everything you've heard about Kings Cross is probably true – it retains a sleazy, cannibalistic aura – but the vague sense of menace is more imaginary than real. Sometimes the razzle-dazzle has a sideshow appeal; sometimes walking up Darlinghurst Rd promotes pity. Either way, it's never boring.

Darlinghurst is less clichéd in its debauchery, but Darlinghursters are still the masters of their own nihilistic, pill-popping universe. Excellent coffee shops, pubs, bars and eateries line Darlinghurst Rd and Victoria St. The section of Oxford St running through Darlinghurst contains Sydney's best-known gay clubs.

KINGS CROSS, DARLINGHURST & AROUND

Please see over for map

NEIGHBOURHOODS

KINGS CROSS, DARLINGHURST & AROUND

In between Kings Cross and the harbour is Woolloomooloo (show us another word with eight 'o's!). The redevelopment of the wharf here has been a huge success, changing the formerly seedy enclave full of drunks, sailors and drunk sailors to a civilised, gourmet nook. Nearby, Potts Point and Elizabeth Bay are dignified, harbourside suburbs. See p13 for more.

 # SEE

◉ ABORIGINAL FINE ART PRINTS
☎ 9332 1722; www.aboriginalartprints .com.au; 68 Oxford St, Darlinghurst; admission free; 🕑 9am-6pm Mon-Fri, 11am-6pm Sat, by appointment Sun; 🚇 Museum 🚌 378, 380, L82
Lustrous screen prints, rare limited editions, and quality lithographs, etchings and linocuts make this gallery a standout. It houses Sydney's most expansive collection by Australia's leading indigenous artists; look for works by Dennis Nona, Rover Thomas and Rosella Namok.

◉ ARTERY
☎ 9380 8234; www.artery.com.au; Shop 2, 221 Darlinghurst Rd, Darlinghurst; admission free; 🕑 10am-6pm Tue-Fri, to 7pm Thu, to 5pm Sat & Sun; 🚇 Kings Cross 🚌 323-7, 324-5, 333, 389
More art retail than art gallery, this indigenous-art outlet deliberately steers away from the glitzy Sydney gallery scene, sourcing its contemporary, original selections from up-and-coming Central Australian artists. Prices are realistic and affordable; modern indigenous jewellery, hand-woven baskets and gorgeous canvasses start at $25.

◉ ARTSPACE
☎ 9368 1899; www.artspace.org.au; The Gunnery, 43-51 Cowper Wharf Rd, Woolloomooloo; admission free; 🕑 11am-5pm Tue-Sat; 🚌 311; ♿
Artspace is spacey; the eternal quest is to fill the void with vigorous, engaging Australian and international contemporary art. Things here are decidedly avant-garde – expect lots of conceptual pieces, a/v installations and new-media masterpieces.

◉ ELIZABETH BAY HOUSE
☎ 9356 3022; www.hht.net.au; 7 Onslow Ave, Elizabeth Bay; admission $8/4; 🕑 10am-4.30pm Tue-Sun; 🚇 Kings Cross 🚌 311
Built between 1835 and 1839 for Colonial Secretary Alexander Macleay, this elegant neoclassical mansion was the finest house in the colony. Ugly 20th-century apartments now surround it, but the exquisite oval salon and stairwell are timeless architectural delights. Wheelchair access to ground floor only.

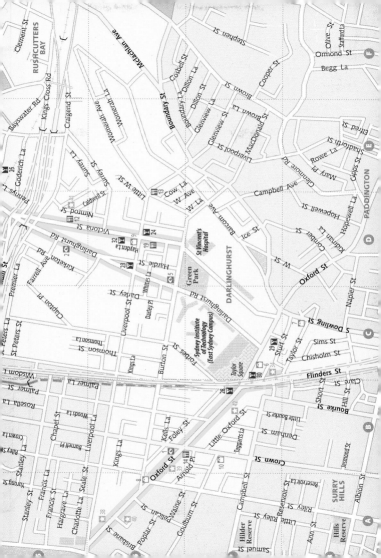

SYDNEY JEWISH MUSEUM

☎ 9360 7999; www.sydneyjewish museum.com.au; 148 Darlinghurst Rd, Darlinghurst; admission $10/7; ✛ 10am-4pm Sun-Thu, to 2pm Fri, closed Jewish holidays; ® Kings Cross ☒ 311, 389; &

Created as a living memorial to the Holocaust, the Sydney Jewish Museum examines Australian Jewish history, culture and tradition from the time of the First Fleet to the present day.

SHOP

BOOKSHOP *Bookshop*

☎ 9331 1103; www.thebookshop .com.au; 207 Oxford St, Darlinghurst; ✛ 10am-10pm Mon-Wed, to 11pm Thu, 11am-midnight Fri & Sat, 11am-11pm Sun; ☒ 378, 380, 389

The obvious name doesn't inspire, but this large, fastidious gay and lesbian bookshop on the Oxford St 'Golden Mile' is far from lacklustre. Titles range from queer theory through to erotica, magazines and Australian fiction.

CAPITAL L *Fashion*

☎ 9361 0111; www.capital-l.com; 333 South Dowling St, Darlinghurst; ✛ 11am-6pm Mon-Fri, to 8pm Thu, 10am-6pm Sat, noon-5pm Sun; ☒ 378, 380, 389

Owner Louise stocks 52 funky up-and-coming designers to complement those already in the limelight. Hip sales staff break from tradition and actually help you find and try on clothes by local talents like Alice McCall.

CENTRAL STATION *Music*

☎ 9361 5222; www.centralstationsyd ney.com.au; 46a Oxford St, Darlinghurst; ✛ 10am-7pm Mon-Fri, to 9pm Thu, to 6pm Sat, noon-6pm Sun; ® Museum ☒ 378, 380, 389

Clubbers, DJs and dance music aficionados pile into this stalwart store for the latest local and overseas vinyl. Breaks, deep-house, disco and electro music dominate; dance-party tickets and imported magazines also make the grade. Pick up a turntable or two for your private DJ endeavours.

SEDITION *Music*

☎ 9331 8832; 275 Victoria St, Darlinghurst; ✛ 9am-6pm Mon-Sat; ® Kings Cross ☒ 323-7, 324-5, 333

Michael the barber will give you a $20 short back 'n' sides while you give jazz, reggae and classic rock records a try-before-you-buy listen and attempt to ignore the wall of '60s *Playboy* centrefolds. He also sells weird books, cult videos and other kooky stuff – maybe a 'How to Play Banjo' guide is up your alley.

WHEELS & DOLL BABY *Fashion*

☎ 9361 3286; www.wheelsanddollbaby .com; 259 Crown St, Darlinghurst;

V

NEIGHBOURHOODS

⏰ 10am-6pm Mon-Sat, to 8pm Thu, noon-5pm Sun; 🚇 Museum Ⓜ World Square 🚌 308-10, 343
'Clothes to snare a millionaire' is the name of the game here, and what a wicked, wicked game it is. Lace, leather and leopard-print; studs, suspenders and satin. Tight-wrapped and trussed-up, it won't just be the millionaires who'll be looking your way.

EAT

🍴 AKI'S *Indian* $$
☎ 9332 4600; www.akisindian.com.au; 1 The Wharf, Cowper Wharf Rd, Woolloomooloo; ⏰ noon-3pm Sun-Fri, 6pm-late daily; 🚌 311; ♿ Ⓥ
The first cab off the rank as you walk onto Woolloomooloo's

wharf is Aki's. And you need walk no further: this is beautifully presented, intuitively constructed high-Indian cuisine, supplemented by a six-page wine list showcasing local and international drops by the glass or bottle. The Kerala chilli beef is a simmering sensation.

🍴 BAR COLUZZI *Café* $
☎ 9380 5420; 322 Victoria St, Darlinghurst; ⏰ 5am-7pm; 🚇 Kings Cross 🚌 323-7, 324-5, 389; Ⓥ ♿
Legendary Coluzzi has been infusing Darlinghurst with caffeine for 50 years. The food is fine, but what you're here for is the spoon-standing-up-straight-in-the-cup coffee.

KINGS CROSS, DARLINGHURST & AROUND

Caffeine junkies, get your fix at Bar Coluzzi

🍴 BILLS *Mod Oz* $$

☎ 9360 9631; www.bills.com.au;
433 Liverpool St, Darlinghurst;
🕐 7.30am-3pm daily, 6-10.30pm
Mon-Sat; 🚌 373, 377, 380, 389, 399;
Ⓥ ♿

Sydneysiders adore Bill Granger's sunny eatery with its large, newspaper-strewn communal table. Dishes like sweetcorn fritters with roast tomato, spinach and bacon are equally adorable. Can't get a seat? Head for the other branches of **bills** Surry Hills (Map p89, C3; ☎ 9360 4762; 359 Crown St) Woollahra (Map p111, E3; ☎ 9328 7997; 118 Queen St).

🍴 CLOVE *Indian* $$

☎ 9361 0980; fax 9361 0987;
249 Crown St, Darlinghurst; 🕐 11.30am-3pm Mon-Fri (bookings only), 5.30-11pm Mon-Thu, to 11.30pm Fri & Sat; 🚉 Museum Ⓜ World Square 🚌 308-10, 343;
Ⓥ ♿

Owner Nash has been cooking up a mean mountain of curry here for 14 years, filling his tables without so much as a hint of advertising. Word of mouth is a powerful force, almost as powerful as Nash's special lamb shank and chicken curries.

🍴 DOV *Mod Oz* $$

☎ 9368 0600; cafedov@bigpond.com;
Shop 2, 130 Victoria St, Potts Point;
🕐 7am-4pm Mon & Tue, to 10pm Wed-Sat, 8.30am-3pm Sun; 🚉 Kings Cross
🚌 323-7, 324-5, 389; Ⓥ

It's probably linked to endless nights of party-love, but big breakfasts are something Sydney does well. DOV, the busiest café on Victoria St, does one of the best. If they sleep through breakfast, locals, backpackers, style-mongers and filmmakers squish in for lunch and dinner. The DOV burger reigns supreme.

🍴 FRATELLI PARADISO
Italian $$

☎ 9357 1744; 12-16 Challis Ave, Potts Point 🕐 7am-11pm Mon-Fri, to 5pm Sat & Sun; 🚉 Kings Cross 🚌 311; ♿ Ⓥ

This stylish bistro/bakery has them queuing at the door (especially on weekends). The intimate, mod room showcases seasonal Italian dishes cooked with Mediterranean zing. Lots of busy black-clad waiters, lots of Italian chatter, lots of oversized sunglasses – somehow Rome doesn't seem so far away… No bookings.

🍴 HARRY'S CAFÉ DE WHEELS
Café $

☎ 9357 3074; www.harryscafedewheels .com.au; Cowper Wharf Rd, Woolloomooloo; 🕐 7.30am-1am Sun-Thu, 9am-4am Fri & Sat; 🚌 311; ♿ ♿

For over 50 years, cab drivers, sailors and boozed-up nocturnals have slurred orders for pea-and-pie floaters over Harry's famous counter. Sit on a milk crate overlooking the hulking Woolloomooloo warships and gulp down a 'Tiger' (pie, peas, mashed potatoes and gravy). Deadly.

HUGO'S BAR PIZZA
Italian $$

☎ 9357 4018; www.hugos.com.au; 33 Bayswater Rd, Kings Cross; ⏰ 5pm-2am Mon-Sat, 3pm-2am Sun; 🚆 Kings Cross 🚌 323-7, 324-5, 333; ♿ V

Sassy little brother of Hugo's Lounge upstairs (p104), this indoor/outdoor neighbourhood nook has been seducing pizza fans with its delicious discs and home-style Italian fare. The marble-fronted bar and sunken velvet lounge spell luxury, but the menu won't break the bank. Try the *puttanesca* pizza.

LIBERTINE
Mod Oz/Southeast Asian $$$

☎ 9368 7507; www.libertine.net.au; 1 Kellett St, Kings Cross; ⏰ 6-11pm; 🚆 Kings Cross 🚌 323-7, 324-5, 333; V

Libertine means 'morally dissolute'. Check your moral fibre at the door of this luxuriant, unrestrained wonderland – gold and crimson drapes, lacquered black timbers and chandeliers set the scene for captivating fusion dishes like the house curry (green prawns, squid and butternut pumpkin). Cement your moral decay at the cocktail bar.

OH! CALCUTTA! *Indian* $$$

☎ 9360 3650; www.ohcalcutta.com.au; 251 Victoria St, Darlinghurst; ⏰ 6-10.30pm Mon-Sat; 🚆 Kings Cross 🚌 323-7, 324-5, 333, 389; V

Oh! Goat curry! This place has won more 'Sydney's Best Indian' accolades than you've had vindaloos. Jazz plays as patrons tuck into tandoori quail and duck curry with kipfler potatoes and leeks. Owner Basil is as spicy as his cooking.

OTTO *Italian* $$$

☎ 9368 7488; www.otto.net.au; 8 The Wharf, Cowper Wharf Rd, Woolloomooloo; ⏰ noon-midnight; 🚌 311; ♿ V

Forget the glamorous waterfront location and A-list crowd – what Otto will be remembered for is single-handedly dragging Sydney's Italian cooking into the new century. Dishes like *strozzapreti con gamberi* (artisan pasta with fresh Yamba prawns, tomato, chilli and black olives) define culinary perfection. Bookings essential.

YELLOW *Mod Oz/deli* $$

☎ 9357 3400; fax 9357 3433; 57-59 Macleay St, Potts Point; ⏰ 7.30am-9.30pm Mon-Sat, to 6pm Sun; 🚆 Kings Cross 🚌 311; V ♿

Yes indeed, it's yellow. The cheeriness continues inside where bouncy/touchy/feely staff enthusiastically proffer the finest olive oils, homemade pastas, cakes, quiches, jam, polenta and sausages. The bistro next door throws it all together and comes up with winners. Hey, is that Paul Keating in the corner?

ZINC Café $$

☎ 9358 6777; zincbar@ihug.com.au; 77 Macleay St, Potts Point; ⏱ 7am-4pm daily, 6.30-11pm Tue-Sat; ☒ Kings Cross ☒ 311; V

Zinc's good-looking staff are full of smiles; maybe the new dinner shifts agree with them. But Zinc was built on breakfasts, and the kitchen continues to create too many hard decisions for 8am. The pancakes with ricotta and berry compote, or eggs with sugar-cured salmon?... Both.

▼ DRINK

▼ DARLO BAR Pub

☎ 9331 3672; www.royalsov.com.au; Royal Sovereign Hotel, 306 Liverpool St, Darlinghurst; admission free; ⏱ 10am-midnight Mon-Sat, noon-midnight Sun; ☒ Kings Cross ☒ 323-7, 324-5, 333, 389;

The Darlo's triangular retro room is a magnet for thirsty urban bohemians with something to read or a hankering for pinball or pool. Afterwards, they roll down the hill to the beer garden at the Green Park Hotel (right).

▼ GREEN PARK HOTEL Pub

☎ 9380 5311; greenpark@solotel.com; 360 Victoria St, Darlinghurst; admission free; ⏱ 10am-2am Mon-Fri, noon-2am Sat & Sun; ☒ 373, 377, 380, 389, 399

The ever-rockin' Green Park has pool tables, a beer garden with funky Dr Seuss–inspired lighting and a huge central bar teeming with travellers, gays and pierced locals. Bowie and Queen rule the jukebox.

▼ HUGO'S LOUNGE Bar

☎ 9357 4411; www.hugos.com.au; L1, 33 Bayswater Rd, Kings Cross; admission free Mon-Thu, $10 Fri-Sun; ⏱ 5.30pm-3am Thu-Sat, 8pm-3am Sun; ☒ Kings Cross ☒ 323-7, 324-5, 333

Upper-crust interiors attract a glossy crowd of media celebs conducting histrionic conversations in between mobile-phone calls. If it feels like a CD launch you weren't invited to, head to the terrace for a stiff drink or Hugo's Bar Pizza (p103) downstairs for some tasty respite.

▼ JIMMY LIK'S Bar

☎ 8354 1400; www.jimmyliks.com; 186 Victoria St, Potts Point; admission free; ⏱ 5pm-midnight; ☒ Kings Cross ☒ 323-7, 324-5, 333

Understated and subtle, Jimmy's is very cool, with benches almost as long as the cocktail list (try a Thai-hewn Mekong Mary with chilli

NEIGHBOURHOODS

KINGS CROSS, DARLINGHURST & AROUND

Drink in the understated atmosphere at Jimmy Lik's

nam jim). Jimmy's Thai restaurant is next door – there's usually a wait for a seat, but with tasty bar snacks available, what's the hurry?

OLD FITZROY HOTEL *Pub*
☎ 9356 3848; www.oldfitzroy.com.au; 129 Dowling St, Woolloomooloo; ⏲ 11am-midnight Mon-Sat, 3-10pm Sun; 🚇 Kings Cross 🚌 311, 323-7, 324-5, 333
Is it a pub? A theatre? A bistro? Actually it's all three. Grab a bowl of laksa, assess the acting talent of tomorrow and wash it all down with a beer ($35 the lot). The outdoor deck is unbeatable on a steamy summer night.

OXFORD HOTEL *Pub*
☎ 9331 3467; www.theoxfordhotel.com.au; 134 Oxford St, Darlinghurst; admission free; ⏲ 24hr downstairs, Gilligan's 5pm-late, Ginger's 6pm-late Wed-Sat; 🚌 378, 380, 389
Big and beige, the ever-lovin' Oxford is a Taylor Sq beacon. Downstairs it's beer-swilling and mannish. First-floor Gilligan's serves luxe cocktails; top-floor Ginger's has indulgent lounge service. Post-dance-party crowds heave and sway. Wheelchair access downstairs only.

NEIGHBOURHOODS

KINGS CROSS, DARLINGHURST & AROUND

▼ RUBY RABBIT *Bar*

☎ 9332 3197; www.rubyrabbit.com.au; 231 Oxford St, Darlinghurst; admission $10-15; ☽ 9pm-late Thu-Sun; 🚍 378, 380, 389

WOW! What a cool bar. The owners have spared no expense on the interiors, coming up with a design best described as Alice in Wonderland tickles Austin Powers while kissing Britt Ekland in the Palace of Versailles (if you know what we mean). Damn funky, and damn difficult to get into – dress to the nines.

▼ SOL'S DECK BAR *Bar*

☎ 9360 8868; 191 Oxford St, Darlinghurst; admission free Mon-Wed, $5 Thu-Sun; ☽ restaurant 11am-late, bar 8pm-late; 🚍 378, 380, 389; ♿

When you drag your bones out of bed at whatever pm, boot it down to Sol's for a beer, some tapas and a perv over Taylor Sq. The cocktail bar fires up later on with resident DJs Sista P and Renae Stanton. Lipstick ladies love Friday night's 'Bitch' session.

▼ TILBURY HOTEL *Pub*

☎ 9368 1955; www.tilburyhotel.com.au; 12-18 Nicholson St, Woolloomooloo; admission free; ☽ 8am-midnight Mon-Fri, from 9am Sat, from 10am Sun; 🚍 311

Once the dank domain of burly sailors and salty ne'er-do-wells,

the Tilbury now sparkles on Sydney's social scene. Yuppies, yachties, suits, gays and straights populate the light, bright interiors. The bistro and beer garden are packed on weekends, and sailors can still get a beer.

▼ VICTORIA ROOM *Bar*

☎ 9357 4488; www.thevictoriaroom.com; L1, 235 Victoria St, Darlinghurst; admission free; ☽ 6pm-midnight Tue-Thu, to 2am Fri & Sat, 2pm-midnight Sun; 🚉 Kings Cross 🚍 323-7, 324-5, 333, 389

Plush chesterfields, Art Nouveau wallpaper, dark-wood panelling and bamboo screens – the Victoria Room is the spoilt love child of a 1920s Bombay gin palace and a Hong Kong opium den. Don your white linen suit and panama and order a Raspberry Debonair at the bar.

▼ WATER BAR *Bar*

☎ 9331 9000; www.tajhotels.com/sydney; BLUE Sydney, 6 Cowper Wharf Rd, Woolloomooloo; admission free; ☽ 4pm-midnight, to 10pm Sun & Mon; 🚍 311; ♿

Time is meaningless and escape is pointless here (especially after a few martinis). The lofty, romantic space sucks you in to its pink-love world of candles, corners, deep lounges and ottomans as big as beds. Great for business (if you really must), but better for lurve.

PLAY

ARQ *Club*
☎ 9380 8700; www.arqsydney.com.au; 16 Flinders St, Darlinghurst; admission Fri/Sat/Sun $10/20/5, Thu free; ⏱ 9pm-6am Thu & Fri, 10pm-9am Sat, 9pm-9am Sun; 🚌 378, 380, 389; ♿
If Noah had to fill his Arq with groovy, gay clubbers, he'd head here with a big net and some tranquillisers. This flash megaclub has a cocktail bar, recovery room and two dance floors with hi-energy house, drag shows and a hyperactive smoke machine.

CANDYS APARTMENT *Club*
☎ 9380 5600; www.candys.com.au; 22 Bayswater Rd, Kings Cross; admission $10-15; ⏱ 8pm-late Thu-Sun; 🚉 Kings Cross 🚌 323-7, 324-5, 333
An unpretentious, grungy club, unique in its decision to let ugly people in the door. The music is good and no one really bothers about anything other than having a few drinks, a dance and a good time. Occasional live acts.

DARLINGHURST THEATRE COMPANY *Theatre*
☎ 8356 9987; www.darlinghursttheatre.com; 19 Greenknowe Ave, Potts Point; tickets $28/22; ⏱ box office 6-10pm Tue-Sat, 4-7pm Sun; 🚉 Kings Cross 🚌 311
The DTC brings clever, pithy and intelligent Australian scripts to life in its intimate (and allegedly haunted!) Potts Point theatre. The theatre features seats, dressing room mirrors, lighting, and the original bar top from the old Her Majesty's Theatre in Haymarket.

DESTINY TOURS *Organised tour*
☎ 0414 232 244, 9943 0167; www.destinytours.com.au; departs cnr Amos La & Elizabeth Bay Rd, Kings Cross; tours $77; ⏱ 8-10.30pm; 🚉 Kings Cross
Under the cover of darkness, climb into 'Elvira' – a black 1967 Cadillac hearse – and embark on a sexy, sleazy, fun and factual tour of Sydney's seamy underbelly. Sordid tales of convicts, crime, celebrities, scandals and ghosts unfurl as you rattle the skeletons in Sydney's closet.

EXCHANGE HOTEL *Club*
☎ 9331 2956; www.qbar.com.au, www.pashpresents.com; 34-44 Oxford St, Darlinghurst; admission Q bar free-$20, Spectrum $7-25, Phoenix $5-10, Exchange free; ⏱ Q Bar & Phoenix 10pm-late Wed-Sun, Spectrum 8pm-late Wed-Sun, Exchange 10am-4am Mon-Fri, 9am-6am Sat & Sun; 🚉 Museum 🚌 378, 380, 389
There's a whole mess of venues here, mashed together under one roof: Q Bar pumps hot house seven nights a week; Spectrum is an alt-indie club with live bands; sticky,

Tacky and seedy just add to the vibe at Kings Cross

sexy, claustrophobic Phoenix is home to alternative gay clubbers. Sandwiched in between, the Exchange is a regulation beery pub.

⭐ MIDNIGHT SHIFT *Club*
☎ 9360 4319; www.themidnightshift .com; 85 Oxford St, Darlinghurst; admission video bar free, club $10-20; ⏱ video bar noon-late Mon-Fri, from 3pm Sun, club 11pm-late Fri & Sat; 🚇 Museum 🚌 378, 380, 389

Sydney's perennial good-time boy palace packs in everyone from beefcakes to drags. The grog is cheap, the patrons messy, Kylie rules and mankind chalks its collective cue by the pool tables. Pick up a pick-up card at the bar to help with introductions ('I'm easy…but it looks like you're hard…').

⭐ SLIDE *Club*
☎ 8915 1899; www.slide.com.au; 41 Oxford St, Darlinghurst; admission Wed & Thu free, Fri/Sat after 10pm $5/10; ⏱ 6pm-3am Wed & Thu, 5pm-4am Fri, 7pm-4am Sat & Sun; 🚇 Museum 🚌 378, 380, 389; ♿

Slide inside Slide, a gorgeously converted banking chamber where a colourful crowd of sexy gays and straights shimmy across polished concrete between plush booths and the central bar. If the sound and vision overwhelms, spy yourself a candidate from the mezzanine.

⭐ STABLES THEATRE *Theatre*
☎ **9361 3817, tickets 1300 306 776; www.griffintheatre.com.au; 10 Nimrod St, Darlinghurst; tickets from $22;** ⏱ **box office 1hr before shows;** 🚇 **Kings Cross** 🚌 **323-7, 324-5, 333, 389**
In the 19th century this place was knee-high in horse dung; now it's home to the critically acclaimed Griffin Theatre Co, dedicated to nurturing new writers and performing experimental works by contemporary Australian playwrights. Book online, by phone or at the box office an hour before the show.

⭐ STONEWALL HOTEL *Club*
☎ **9360 1963; www.stonewallhotel .com; 175 Oxford St, Darlinghurst; admission free;** ⏱ **11am-6am;** 🚌 **378, 380, 389**
Nicknamed 'Stonehenge' by those who think it's archaic (gay druids?), the Stonewall has three levels of bars and dance floors. Cabaret, karaoke and games nights spice things up – Wednesday's 'Malebox' is a sure-fire way to bag yourself a boy.

⭐ SYDNEY BY DIVA *Organised tour*
☎ **9360 5557; www.sydneybydiva .au; tours depart Oxford Hotel, Taylor Sq, Darlinghurst; tours $100;** ⏱ **2pm, 5pm & 8pm subject to bookings;** 🚌 **378, 380, 389**
All aboard for a truly camp, three-hour, 'rosé-tinted' drag queen comic tour of Sydney, taking in the Opera House, Bondi Beach and a drag show at the Imperial Hotel, home of *Priscilla, Queen of the Desert.*

⭐ TONIC LOUNGE *Club*
☎ **8354 1544; www.toniclounge.com .au; 62-64 Kellett St, Kings Cross; admission $5-10;** ⏱ **9pm-late Fri-Sun;** 🚇 **Kings Cross** 🚌 **323-7, 324-5, 333**
Just the tonic for snooty Sydney – a laid-back, clubby boudoir in a black-and-purple terrace house that feels more like someone's living room than anything hi-tech or *haute couture*. The fact that it's so un-Sydney attracts people who are also un-Sydney – expect backpackers aplenty.

⭐ YU *Club*
☎ **9358 65117; www.yu.com.au; 171 Victoria St, Potts Point; admission Fri/Sat/Sun $15/20/10;** ⏱ **10pm-6am Fri-Sun;** 🚇 **Kings Cross** 🚌 **323-7, 324-5, 333**
Debut the sassy new eastern suburbs you at Yu. Sydney's best house DJs and vocal MCs spin hip-hop, nu-skool, vocal and funky house in three rooms divided by sliding video screens. 'Piccadilly Sundays' sessions kick til you can't take no mo'. Upstairs is Soho Bar – an Art Deco space where visiting celebs like to shoot pool.

>PADDINGTON & WOOLLAHRA

Paddington, aka 'Paddo', is a steep, leafy suburb of restored terrace houses. Rugged bushland until the 1860s, Paddo was built for aspiring Victorian artisans, but after WWII it became Australia's worst slum. In the 1960s, renewed passion for Victorian architecture dragged Paddington back from the brink; by the '90s, real estate was out of reach for all but the lucky and the loaded.

Today, fashionable types drift between Oxford St's designer shops, chic restaurants and galleries. The suburb's flamboyant spirit comes courtesy of a vibrant gay community; Taylor Square on Oxford St is gay Sydney's decadent nucleus. Just north of Oxford St is Five Ways, a neighbourhood hotspot. At the eastern end of Oxford St is Centennial Park, Sydney's biggest park.

Woollahra is upper-crust Sydney at its finest. Leafy streets, mansions, wall-to-wall BMWs and expensive antique shops. Maybe this is your bag; maybe it isn't – whatever your inclination, spending an afternoon here is socially enlightening.

PADDINGTON & WOOLLAHRA

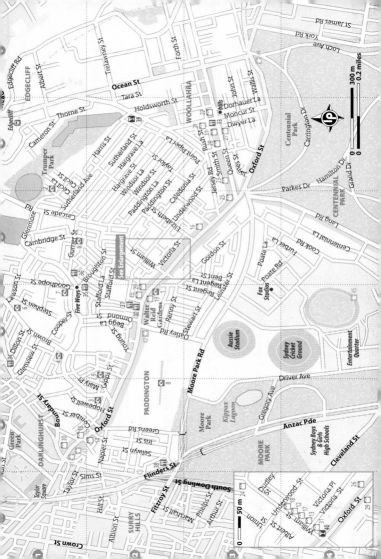

SEE

AUSTRALIAN CENTRE FOR PHOTOGRAPHY
☎ 9332 1455; www.acp.au.com; 257 Oxford St, Paddington; admission free; ☽ 11am-6pm Tue-Sun; ☐ 378, 380, 389

The nonprofit ACP exhibits the photographic gems of renowned Sydney and international photographers. They're particularly passionate about photomedia, video and digital imaging works, their displays extending into their new multiexhibition space next door.

AUSTRALIAN GALLERIES
☎ 9360 5177; www.australiangalleries .com.au; 15 Roylston St, Paddington; admission free; ☽ 10am-6pm Mon-Sat; ☐ 378, 380, 389

Contemporary Australian painting and sculpture for cashed-up collectors; A-list artists have been jostling to hang their wares here for 50 years. Works on paper feature at the **Glenmore Rd branch** (☎ 9380 8744; 24 Glenmore Rd; ☽ 10am-6pm Tue-Sat, noon-5pm Sun).

CERAMIC ART GALLERY
☎ 9361 5286; www.ceramicart .com.au/gallery/gallery.htm; 120 Glenmore Rd, Paddington; admission free; ☽ 11am-5pm Thu-Mon; ☐ 378, 380, 389

Pushing clay to its rightful extremes (is there anything else as deliciously malleable?), exhibits at the Ceramic Art Gallery range from exquisite bowls and eggshell-thin vases to chunky slabs of abstract madness worth starting conversations over.

HOGARTH GALLERIES
☎ 9360 6839; www.aboriginalart centres.com; 7 Walker La, Paddington; admission free; ☽ 10am-5pm Tue-Sat; ☐ 378, 380, 389

A cultural beacon in an obscure Paddington laneway, Hogarth has supported and promoted Aboriginal art since 1972. Honouring established artists and sourcing up-and-comers, Hogarth exhibits contemporary dot paintings, basketry, framed prints, fabrics, spears and didgeridoos.

NEILD AVENUE MAZE
☎ 9391 7000; cnr Neild Ave & Gosbell St, Paddington; admission free; ☐ 378, 380, 389; ⚹

This tiny maze of impeccably trimmed, thigh-high hedges hides behind a gargantuan plane tree on a Paddington back street, squished into a cranny between a gallery and someone's back fence. It mightn't take you forever to find your way through, but it'll add a smile to your day.

SHERMAN GALLERIES

☎ 9331 1112; www.shermangalleries
.com.au; 16-20 Goodhope St, Paddington;
admission free; ⏰ 10am-6pm Tue-Fri,
11am-6pm Sat; 🚌 378, 380, 389; ♿

Big-time Australian artists command big-time prices inside this schmick sculpture and contemporary art salon. Polished concrete floors, spot-lit white walls and a sculpture garden make the prospect of owning something by Daniel Crooks, Guan Wei or Janet Lawrence seem oddly attainable.

VICTORIA BARRACKS

☎ 9339 3170; www.awm.gov.au; cnr
Oxford St & Greens Rd, Paddington; tour
free, museum $2/1; ⏰ tour 10am Thu,
museum 10am-4pm Thu & Sun, closed
Dec-Feb; 🚌 378, 380, 389; ♿

A manicured malarial vision from the peak of the British Empire, these Georgian buildings have been called the finest in the colonies. Thursday's tours take in a flag-raising ceremony, marching band (subject to availability) and the paraphernalia-packed war museum.

WAGNER ART GALLERY

☎ 9360 6069; www.wagnerartgallery
.com.au; 39 Gurner St, Paddington; admission free; ⏰ 10.30am-6pm Mon-Sat,
1-6pm Sun; 🚌 378, 380, 389

Think Boyd, Lindsay, Nolan and Friend. Think top dollar. Think champagne, turtlenecked, lah-de-dah openings (6pm to 8pm one Tuesday per month). Wagner is one of the oldest galleries in Paddington, its maturity reflected in its composed atmosphere and high-brow decency.

SHOP

ARIEL *Bookshop*

☎ 9332 4581; www.arielbooks.com
.au; 42 Oxford St, Paddington; ⏰ 9am-
midnight; 🚌 378, 380, 389

Furtive artists, photographers, architects and students roam Ariel's aisles late into the night. 'Underculture' is the thrust here – glossy art, film, fashion and design books, along with kids' books, travel guides and a queer literature section. Browse before a movie at the Academy Twin Cinema (p120) across the road.

ARTE FLOWERS *Homewares*

☎ 9328 0402; www.arteflowers.com;
112 Queen St, Woollahra; ⏰ 10am-
5.30pm Mon-Fri, 9.30am-5.30pm Sat,
10am-5pm Sun; 🚌 378, 380, 389

Part gift shop, part tea rooms, this airy space carries French skincare products, faux-flowers, candles, photo frames and chic gardening tools. After all that shopping, enjoy a cup of Australian husk tea and a slice of lemon tart at the communal table.

NEIGHBOURHOODS

PADDINGTON & WOOLLAHRA

DIVINE DESIGNERS

Paddington is ripe with fab, flimsy Australian creations for size-six disciples of international style:

Bracewell (☎ 9331 5844; www.bracewell.com.au; 274 Oxford St, Paddington; ⏱ 10am-6pm Mon-Fri, to 8pm Thu, 10am-5pm Sat, noon-5pm Sun; 🚌 378, 380, 389) Sexy, structured and sassy; Mavi and Sass & Bide jeans.

Lisa Ho (☎ 9360 2345; www.lisaho.com.au; 2a Queen St, Woollahra; ⏱ 10am-6pm Mon-Sat, to 8pm Thu, 11am-5pm Sun; 🚌 378, 380, 389) Sheer party frocks for the social whirlwind that is your life.

Morrissey (☎ 9380 7422; www.morrissey.net.au; 372 Oxford St, Paddington; ⏱ 10am-6pm Mon-Sat, to 8pm Thu, 11am-5pm Sun; 🚌 378, 380, 389) Attention high-heeled amber-tan babes: bring your gold credit card.

🏠 BELINDA *Fashion*
☎ 9387 8728; www.belinda.com.au; 39 William St, Paddington; ⏱ 10am-6pm Mon-Sat, noon-5pm Sun; 🚌 378, 380, 389
Belinda stocks a tightly edited collection of Australian designers and expensive international imports. Its second, mildly less wallet-threatening store the **Corner Shop** (☎ 9380 9828; 43 William St) is a treasure-trove of funky Australian stuff. There's also **Belinda Menswear** (☎ 9380 8873; 29 William St).

🏠 BERKELOUW BOOKS
Bookshop
☎ 9360 3200; www.berkelouw.com.au; 19 Oxford St, Paddington; ⏱ 9am-midnight; 🚌 378, 380, 389
Expecting the dank aroma of second-hand books? Forget it! Follow your nose up to the café, then browse through three floors of preloved tomes, new releases,

antique maps and Australia's largest collection of rare books.

🏠 CALIBRE *Fashion*
☎ 9380 5993; www.calibreclothing.com.au; 398 Oxford St, Paddington; ⏱ 9.30am-6pm Mon-Sat, to 8pm Thu, 10am-6pm Sat, 11am-5pm Sun; 🚌 378, 380, 389
Hip, high-calibre Calibre fills the wardrobes of Sydney's power players with schmick suits in seasonal fabrics and colours, plus Gucci sunnies, Costume National shoes, YSL ties and Samsonite briefcases. Gordon Gecko eat your heart out.

🏠 COLLETTE DINNIGAN
Fashion
☎ 9360 6691; www.collettedinnigan.com; 33 William St, Paddington; ⏱ 10am-6pm Mon-Sat, noon-5pm Sun; 🚌 378, 380, 389
This shop's sanded floors, French drapes and wrought-iron staircase

are a sexy backdrop for Collette Dinnigan's flouncy beaded dresses. Hollywood's Aussie gals flock here whenever they need a new frock (Nicole or Naomi might be in the next change room).

🏠 DINOSAUR DESIGNS
Jewellery

☎ 9361 3776; www.dinosaurdesigns
.com.au; 339 Oxford St, Paddington;
🕙 10am-6pm Mon-Sat, noon-5pm Sun;
🚌 378, 380, 389

If Fred and Barney opened a jewellery store, this is what it would look like. Oversized, jewel-coloured, translucent-resin bangles and baubles sit among technicoloured vases and bowls and chunky sterling-silver rings and necklaces.

🏠 FOLKWAYS *Music*

☎ 9361 3980; info@folkways.com.au;
282 Oxford St, Paddington; 🕙 9am-6pm

Mon-Sat, to 9pm Thu, 11am-6pm Sun;
🚌 378, 380, 389

If Mongolian throat singers rock your world, then long-established Folkways – Sydney's premier stockist of world music CDs – is your spiritual home. Expect pressings from Central Asia to the central Australian desert and an extensive selection of jazz and blues.

🏠 JONES THE GROCER *Food & drink*

☎ 9362 1222; www.jonesthegrocer
.com; 68 Moncur St, Woollahra;
🕙 7.30am-5.30pm Mon-Sat, 9am-5pm Sun; 🚌 378, 380, 389

Bob the Builder, Jones the Grocer – some things just make sense. JTG offers high-end groceries, cookbooks and gourmet goodies galore. Munch into a caramel slice with a serious coffee at the café, then double-wrap

Sample the gourmet wares at Jones the Grocer

some double brie and hotfoot it to Centennial Park for a picnic.

⬜ KIDSTUFF *Toy shop*

☎ 9363 2838; www.kidstuff.com.au; 126a Queen St, Woollahra; 🕙 9.30am-5.30pm Mon-Sat, 9am-5pm Sun; 🚌 378, 380, 389

Parents seem relieved to discover this small, vaguely hippie shop filled with educational, traditional, low-tech toys and games. Aiming to engage and expand kids' minds, well-known brands mix with costumes, musical instruments, soft toys, dolls houses and magnetic fridge letters (teach them how to spell 'p-l-a-y-s-t-a-t-i-o-n').

⬜ LEE HARDCASTLE ANTIQUES *Antiques*

☎ 9362 0935; lee.hardcastle@bigpond .com; 28 Queen St, Woollahra; 🕙 10am-5pm Mon-Sat; 🚌 378, 380, 389

Bordering on bizarre, this shop is more like a natural-history museum than an antique dealer. 18th- and early 19th-century taxidermy (zebras, warthogs, black bears and deer) jostle for position with whale ribs, grandfather clocks and walnut wardrobes.

⬜ LEONA EDMISTON *Fashion*

☎ 9331 7033; www.leonaedmiston .com; 88 William St, Paddington; 🕙 10am-6pm Mon-Fri, to 5pm Sat, noon-4pm Sun; 🚌 378, 380, 389

With two new stores in LA, Leona Edmiston clearly knows a thing or two about dresses. Her sassy designs have been described as exuberantly feminine, flirtatious and fun, cut from the best cottons, silks and jerseys in colours that range from luscious, sophisticated reds to pinstripes and polka dots.

⬜ ORSON & BLAKE *Homewares*

☎ 9326 1155; www.orsonandblake .com.au; 83-85 Queen St, Woollahra; 🕙 9.30am-5.30pm Mon-Sat, noon-5pm Sun; 🚌 378, 380, 389

Sydney's most stylin' homewares emporium will make your house look cool even if you're not – everything from notepads to garden statues at the height of chic. Head upstairs for clothes by top-notch Australian and Kiwi designers plus opulent scarves, handbags and jewellery. There's more clothing at their nearby **store** (78 Queen St).

⬜ PADDINGTON MARKET *Market*

☎ 9331 2923; www.paddingtonmarkets .com.au; 395 Oxford St, Paddington; 🕙 10am-4pm Sat, to 5pm summer; 🚌 378, 380, 389

Join the meandering throngs for a foot massage, tarot reading or funky shirt to wear clubbing that night. Sydney's most-attended

Feminine meets fun at Leona Edmiston

weekend market congregates around Paddington Uniting Church, coughing up everything from vintage clothes and hip fashions to jewellery, books, massage and palmistry. Parking is a misery here – take public transport.

VERNE JEWELS Jewellery

☎ 9361 3669; vernjewels@hotmail.com; 36b Oxford St, Paddington; 🕙 10am-5pm Mon-Sat; 🚌 378, 380, 389
With an exquisite eye and a wry sense of history, Nicholas Bullough (no, he's not Verne, that's a joke – Jules Verne, get it?) assembles the artefacts, stones, pearls

NEIGHBOURHOODS

PADDINGTON & WOOLLAHRA

and gems he buys around the world and comes up with winners every time.

🔲 VICTORIA SPRING
Jewellery

☎ 9331 7862; www.victoriaspring designs.com.au; 5 William St, Paddington; 🕒 10am-6pm Mon-Sat, to 7pm Thu; 🚍 378, 380, 389

Addicted to delicately beaded, vintage-style costume jewellery, Paddington princesses have followed Victoria Spring from its Oxford St beginnings to haughtier William St. Equally delectable antique cushions and delicate china teapots complete the femme-fatale fantasy.

🍴 EAT

🍴 ARTHUR'S PIZZA
Italian $$

☎ 9332 2220; 260 Oxford St, Paddington; 🕒 5pm-midnight Mon-Fri, noon-midnight Sat & Sun; 🚍 378, 380, 389; V 🔥

For some reason Arthur's sign was originally installed upside down. Then some do-gooder turned it right-way-up. Now it's topsy-turvy again. Immune to this sign-writing schizophrenia, Art's pizzas continue to impress. Try the 'Zorro' (olives, ricotta, red onion, spinach and semidried tomato).

🍴 BISTRO MONCUR
French $$$

☎ 9363 2519; www.bistromoncur .au; 116 Queen St, Woollahra; 🕒 noon-3pm Thu-Sun, 6-10.30pm daily, to 9pm Sun; 🚍 378, 380, 389; V

Mini-moguls and luncheon ladies while away afternoons below Bistro Moncur's vaulted ceilings and Matisse-esque murals. Dishes like blue swimmer crab omelette are ingrained in Sydney's culinary lexicon. The wine list will make you want to take up mogulling too.

🍴 BUON RICORDO *Italian* $$$

☎ 9360 6729; www.buonricordo .com.au; 108 Boundary St, Paddington; 🕒 noon-2.30pm Fri & Sat, 6.30-10.30pm Tue-Sat, supper 'til midnight; 🚍 378, 380, 389; V

Remember the good old days, when local restaurateurs knew you well enough to select your meal for you? Well, Buon Ricordo is very 'good old days'. Let bearded chef Armando Percuoco decide whether you want the *zuppa di pesce* or the *tagliata con rucola*. The best Italian in Sydney? Reservations essential.

🍴 GUSTO *Café/deli* $

☎ 9361 5640; fax 9328 2083; 2a Heely St, Five Ways, Paddington; 🕒 7am-8pm Mon-Sat, 7.30am-8pm Sun; 🚍 378, 380, 389; 🔥 V

Busy to the point of embarrassment for the surrounding busi-

When in Sydney, eat with Gusto

nesses, Gusto does things with gusto. Breakfast rolls (egg, ham, tomato and hollandaise on an on- ion roll) nourish skinny actresses on the footpath tables, while the deli doles out cheeses, pesto, hams and olives with enthused abandon.

🍴 **LA GERBE D'OR**
French café $
☎ 9331 1070; 255 Glenmore Rd, Five Ways, Paddington; 🕑 7am-7pm Tue-Fri, to 6pm Sat, to 4pm Sun; 🚌 378, 380, 389; Ⓥ ♿
Sydney's most-loved patisserie, La Gerbe d'Or (pronunciation:

with *theek* Parisian accent) has been baking mouth-watering French breads, cakes, pastries and quiches for 25 years. The chunky beef-and-burgundy pies are legendary.

▥ PERRY LANE CAFÉ
Café $

☎ 9358 5259; fax 9969 9318; 1 Perry La, Paddington; ⏲ 7.30am-4.30pm Mon-Sat; ▤ 378, 380, 389; Ⅴ ♿

Follow the freeway-style signs down Perry La to this unexpected little café and escape the Oxford St hubbub for a while. There's great coffee, breakfast burritos and it's very kid- and tea-drinker-friendly (each with dedicated menu pages). The lemon chicken Turkish sandwich with chilli mayonnaise is a doozey.

▥ WILDRICE *Thai* $$

☎ /fax 8354 0088; Shop 1, 160 Flinders St, Paddington; ⏲ 6.30-10.30pm Mon-Sat; ▤ L94, 333, 373, 377, 392; Ⅴ

In Paddington's obscure western reaches, Wildrice is a glorious exaltation of contemporary Thai cooking. Rice arrives in moulded conical mounds, which you smother with red chicken-breast curry and grilled sweet-chilli scampi. Coriander by the bushel; absolutely sensational.

▾ DRINK

▾ LORD DUDLEY HOTEL *Pub*

☎ 9327 5399; www.lorddudley.com.au; 236 Jersey Rd, Woollahra; admission free; ⏲ 11am-11pm Mon-Wed, to midnight Thu-Sat, noon-10pm Sun; ▤ 378, 380, 389

Packed with poncy, scarf-wearing MG drivers and block-shouldered Rugby Union types, the Lord Dudley is as close as Sydney gets to an English pub. Dark woody walls; quality beers by the pint.

▾ PADDINGTON INN *Pub*

☎ 9380 5277; paddingtoninn@solotel.com.au; 338 Oxford St, Paddington; admission free; ⏲ noon-midnight Sun-Thu, to 1am Fri & Sat; ▤ 378, 380, 389

The Paddo's exterior makes stylised use of peeling paint: inside it's all organically-shaped wall nooks, stainless-steel stools and mildly sinister lighting. Good-looking locals elbow around the pool table; the restaurant serves upmarket pub grub.

⭐ PLAY

☆ ACADEMY TWIN CINEMA
Cinema

☎ 9331 3457; www.palacecinemas.com.au; 3a Oxford St, Paddington; tickets $15/12; ⏲ 11am-9.30pm; ▤ 378, 380, 389

Art-house enthusiasts roll up for the Academy's broad selection of independent Australian and international releases and annual Italian, Mardi Gras, French and Spanish film festivals (in February, March, April and May respectively).

⭐ CHAUVEL CINEMA *Cinema*
☎ 9361 5398; www.chauvelcinema.net.au; cnr Oxford St & Oatley Rd, Paddington; tickets $14/12; ☷ 1pm-midnight Mon-Fri, from 11am Sat & Sun; ☐ 378, 380, 389
Inside the historic Paddington Town Hall, the revamped Chauvel's mission statement is to offer distinct and alternative cinema experiences and to foster Sydney's film culture.

⭐ GOODBAR *Club*
☎ 9360 6759; 11a Oxford St, Paddington; admission $10-15; ☷ 9pm-3am Wed, Fri & Sat; ☐ 378, 380, 389
Looking for Mr Goodbar? If he's hiding in this tiny club, it won't take you long to flush him out. No luck? Console yourself with funk, soul, reggae and hip-hop among the taut Paddington bods who make it past the face police on the door.

⭐ MOONLIGHT CINEMA *Cinema*
☎ 1300 551 908; www.moonlight.com.au; Centennial Park, Oxford St, Woollahra; tickets $18/15; ☷ dusk, late Nov–early Mar; ☐ Bondi Junction ☐ 378, 380, 389; ♿ ☃
A mellow way to enjoy a balmy summer evening: bring a rug, a picnic and a mate. The programme includes classics like *Breakfast at Tiffany's*, *Ferris Bueller's Day Off* and *A Clockwork Orange*. Buy tickets online, by phone or at the gate from 7pm (subject to availability).

⭐ SYDNEY COMEDY STORE *Comedy*
☎ 9357 1419; www.comedystore.com.au; Entertainment Quarter, Lang Rd, Moore Park; tickets $15-30; ☷ box office 10am-6pm Mon, to midnight Tue-Sat; ☐ 339, 371-4, 376-7; ♿
This purpose-built comedy hall lures big-time Australian and overseas stand-ups and nurtures new talent with open mike and 'New Comics' nights. US, Irish and Edinburgh Festival performers have 'em rolling in the aisles on a regular basis. Bookings advisable.

>BONDI, BRONTE & COOGEE

In pre-rollerblade days, the flavour of Bondi (🚌 380, 389 from Circular Quay; 🚆 Bondi Junction, then bus 381) came from Jewish, Italian and British immigrants. These days, Bondi (deriving from an Aboriginal word for the sound of the surf) is irresistibly hip – surfers, models, skate punks and tourists surf hedonistically through Campbell Pde's pubs, bars and restaurants. Housing prices on Bondi's treeless slopes have skyrocketed, but the beach remains a priceless constant.

Further south is Bronte (🚌 378 from Railway Sq, via Bondi Junction), a steep-sided beach suburb. The swimming is good, as is the collection of low-key, breezy eateries in what was once an exceedingly uncool shopping strip.

Coogee (🚌 373, 374 from Circular Quay, 372 from Railway Sq; 🚆 Bondi Junction, then bus 313, 314, 353) is further south again, a spacious, popular 'burb that's far enough from the city to be almost self sufficient – beery backpackers fill the Thai takeaways and pubs.

For more on these beaches, see p15. See also the Clifftop Trail (p140).

BONDI, BRONTE & COOGEE

Please see over for map

SEE

BONDI PAVILION

☎ 8362 3400; www.waverley.nsw.gov
.au/info/pavilion; Queen Elizabeth Dr,
Bondi; admission free; 🕓 10am-6pm;
🚌 381 from Bondi Junction, 380, 389
More cultural centre than boat
shed, the 1929 Mediterranean/
Georgian-revival Bondi Pavilion has
change rooms, showers, outdoor
cinema (p131), restaurants, exhibitions, courses and performances.

SHOP

BONDI MARKETS *Market*

☎ 9315 8988; www.bondimarkets
.com.au; Bondi Beach Public School, cnr
Campbell Pde & Warners Ave, Bondi;

WORTH THE TRIP

North of Bondi in Vaucluse is Sydney's last remaining 19th-century
harbourside estate, **Vaucluse House**
(☎ 9388 7922; www.hht.net.au;
Wentworth Rd, Vaucluse; admission
$8/4; 🕓 10am-4.30pm Tue-Sun;
🚌 325). Built in 1828, it's an impos-
ing, turreted specimen of Gothic Australiana on 10 hectares of lush gardens.
Political sabre-rattler and explorer William Charles Wentworth and his family
lived here from 1828 to 1862. Wheelchair access to ground floor only.

🕓 9am-4pm Sun; 🚌 381 from Bondi
Junction, 380, 389
Remember the days of the old
school yard? We used to laugh a

To market, to market: browse the goods at funky Bondi Markets

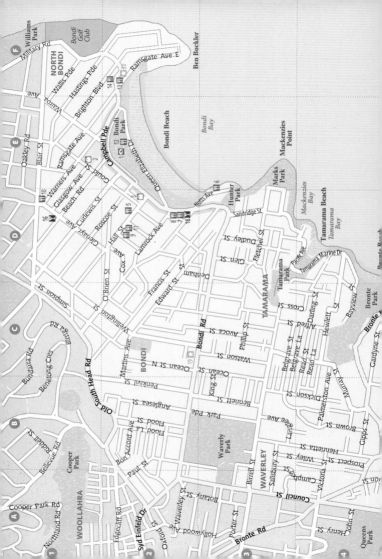

NEIGHBOURHOODS

BONDI, BRONTE & COOGEE

lot… The kids are at the beach on Sundays while their school fills up with Bondi groovers rummaging through funky second-hand clothes and books, hippy beads and earrings, aromatherapy oils, candles, old Cat Stevens records…

📖 MARTIN SMITH BOOKSHOP
Bookshop

☎ 9365 1482; www.martinsmith books
.com.au; 3 Hall St, Bondi; ⏰ 10am-9.30pm;
🚌 381 from Bondi Junction, 380, 389
Do bushy-bushy blonde surfies read books? If the crowds at Martin Smith's are anything to go by, the answer must be yes. This tiny cultural oasis in Bondi's literary desert has more books than space – staff scramble up ladders to get to the top shelves.

🍴 EAT

🍴 BARZURA *Café* $$
☎ 9665 5546; www.barzura.com.au; 64 Carr St, Coogee; ⏰ 7am-11pm;
🚌 353 from Bondi Junction, 372-4, 313-4; ♿ 🅥
Frequented by retired Australian cricketers in dark sunglasses, Barzura's views have to be the best of any café in Sydney (if not the world!). The sunbaked stretch north along Coogee Beach to Bondi is a stunner, as are the deliciously uncomplicated salads,

pides, pasta dishes and generous breakfasts, all served with a smile.

🍴 BLUE ORANGE
Mod Oz/café $$
☎ 9300 9885; www.blueorangeres taurant.com.au; 49 Hall St, Bondi;
⏰ 7am-4.30pm Wed-Sun, 6.30-10.30pm Tue-Sat; 🚌 381 from Bondi Junction, 380, 389; 🅥 ♿
A fave with Hall St regulars and travellers alike, Blue Orange has a casual, sandy vibe and a silly name, belying its delicate, complex cooking. Start with the blue cheese and walnut brûlée, then savour the slow-cooked Flinders Island lamb with roasted eggplant, fetta and mint. Divine.

🍴 BONDI ICEBERGS
Modern Mediterranean $$$
☎ 9365 9000; www.idrb.com; 1 Notts Ave, Bondi; ⏰ noon-midnight Tue-Sat, to 10pm Sun; 🚌 381 from Bondi Junction, 380, 389; ♿ 🅥
Poised above the famous swimming pool, Icebergs' views sweep across the Bondi Beach arc to the sea. Jacketed, bow-tied waiters deliver fresh seafood and steaks cooked with élan. The wine list is superb, and the bar, overlooking the Campbell Pde lights, is never a boring place for a beer. Bow down and feign humility before the mighty Pacific Ocean (don't spill your beer).

Bondi Icebergs is a room with a view

🍴 BONDI SOCIAL *Mod Oz* $$$
☎ 9365 1788; www.bondisocial.com; L1,
38 Campbell Pde, Bondi; 🕑 10am-4pm
Fri-Sun, 6pm-midnight daily; 🚌 381
from Bondi Junction, 380, 389; 🚻 Ⓥ
This cosy, chocolate-coloured,
beach-shaped room opens onto
a deck, from which Pacific views
extend to eternity. Try the honey-
glazed duck with coriander or the
seared yellowfin tuna with paprika,
fennel and salmon caviar. They
also have a mean cocktail menu if
you'd rather just sip and stare.

🍴 GELBISON *Italian* $
☎ 9130 4042; fax 9300 9041; 10
Lamrock Ave, Bondi; 🕑 5-11pm; 🚌 381
from Bondi Junction, 380, 389; Ⓥ 🚻

Legendary enough for a local rock
band to name themselves after it,
Gelbison entertains families, backpackers, locals and visiting movie
stars (is Gelbison an anagram for
Mel Gibson?) with great-value
pizza and pasta. Sit with the surfers over a steaming bowl of prawn
and mushroom fettuccine or a
'magic boot' pizza.

🍴 GERTRUDE & ALICE *Café* $
☎ 9130 5155; gertrudeandalice@big
pond.com; 40 Hall St, Bondi; 🕑 9.30am-
10pm Mon-Fri, 8.30am-10pm Sat & Sun;
🚌 381 from Bondi Junction, 380, 389;
Ⓥ 🚻
This second-hand bookshop/café
is so un-Bondi – there's not a

WORTH THE TRIP

It's been the king of Sydney seafood for so long, you might think **Doyles on the Beach** (☎ 9337 2007; www.doyles .com.au; 11 Marine Pde, Watsons Bay; 🕑 noon-3pm & 6-10pm; 🚤 Watsons Bay 🚢 325; ♿) is resting on its laurels. Nevertheless, they ain't your average fish and chipper, and catching the harbour ferry to Watsons Bay for a seafood lunch is a quintessential Sydney experience.

model or surfer in sight! Students and academics hang out reading, sipping chai tea and acting like Americans in Paris. Join them for a mezze platter and theological discussion around communal tables in shambolic book-lined rooms.

🍴 JED'S FOOD STORE *Café* $

☎ 9365 0022; cnr Glenayr & Warners Aves, North Bondi; 🕑 6.30am-3.30pm; 🚌 381 from Bondi Junction, 380, 389; V ♿

Jed's is so relaxed, you'll feel like you're living in a uni share-house again. Reggae mellows the tattooed staff who sing and groove around; dudes sip coffee outside as kids and dogs run amok. Grab a seat for the Caribbean-style jerked potato scramble and a strong coffee.

🍴 MONGERS *Seafood* $

☎ 9365 2205; fax 9365 2253; 42 Hall St, Bondi; 🕑 11am-9pm; 🚌 381 from Bondi Junction, 380, 389; ♿

Gourmet, grease-free fish and chips for those who are fond of tradition, but not at the expense of their waistline. Grab some low-joule grilled whiting and some thin-cut sweet-potato chips and head for the sand.

🍴 NICK'S *Mod Oz* $$$

☎ 9365 4122; www.nicksbondibeach .com.au; Bondi Pavilion, Queen Elizabeth Dr, Bondi; 🕑 noon-3pm & 6-10pm Mon-Fri, 11am-11pm Sat & Sun; 🚌 381 from Bondi Junction, 380, 389; ♿ ♿

This hugely popular, glass-fronted fishbowl is king of the newly ensconced Bondi Pavilion restaurants. Mood and marketing are 'mainstream chain' (Nick's is one of five around town), but the beach views are bodacious. Try the kangaroo fillet or char-grilled octopus with tomato, fetta and olives.

🍴 NORTH BONDI ITALIAN FOOD *Italian* $$$

☎ 9300 4400; www.idrb.com; 118-20 Ramsgate Ave, North Bondi; 🕑 noon-late Wed-Sun, 6pm-late Mon & Tue; 🚌 381 from Bondi Junction, 380, 389; ♿ V

Expansive windows float your eyes beyond the terrace to the sighing

North Bondi swell. You won't hear any sighs inside (it's all hard surfaces and conversations) but the pasta, seafood, soups and salads engage your other senses. Try the generous wild boar *papardelle*. Wines by the glass.

🍴 SEAN'S PANAROMA
Mod Oz $$$

☎ 9365 4924; www.seanspanaroma
.com.au; 270 Campbell Pde, North Bondi;
⏲ noon-2.30pm Sat & Sun, 6.30-9.30pm
Wed-Sat; 🚌 381 from Bondi Junction,
380, 389; Ⓥ

Ocean vistas, creative dishes, friendly staff and celebrity attendees ensure this hip little noshery's fame. Sean Moran's ever-changing menu lets you eat with the seasons. Suckling pig roasted with cabbage, pear, sweet potato and anise is a winter night's feast. In summer, succumb to seafood.

🍴 SWELL *Mod Oz* $$

☎ 9386 5001; www.swellrestaurant
.com.au; 465 Bronte Rd, Bronte; ⏲ 7am-
10pm; 🚌 378; ♿ Ⓥ

Pull up a pew next to Anthony LaPaglia and/or Jennifer Hawkins for seaside Swell's spanking day-turns-to-night menu. Greet the day with poached eggs, pumpkin, feta and spinach, linger into lunch with a snazzy steak sandwich and return at dinnertime for the salt-and-pepper squid.

🍸 DRINK

🍸 BEACH ROAD HOTEL *Pub*

☎ 9130 7247; brhbondi@bigpond.com;
71 Beach Rd, Bondi; admission free;
⏲ 10am-2.30am Mon-Fri, 9am-12.30am
Sat, 10am-10pm Sun; 🚌 381 from Bondi
Junction, 380, 389; ♿

Weekends at this big, yellow pub are a boisterous multilevel alcoholiday, with Bondi types (bronzed and brooding) and woozy out-of-towners playing pool, drinking beer and digging live bands and DJs. Sleep off your hangover upstairs.

🍸 COOGEE BAY HOTEL *Pub*

☎ 9665 0000; www.coogeebayhotel.com
.au; cnr Coogee Bay Rd & Arden St, Coogee;
admission free; ⏲ 9am-3am Thu-Sat, to
midnight Sun, to 1am Mon-Wed; 🚌 353
from Bondi Junction, 372-4, 313-4; ♿

This rambling, rowdy complex has live music at the legendary Selinas, a beer garden, open-mike nights, comedy, cocktail lounge, sports bar, bistro and bottle shop. Sit on a stool in the window overlooking the beach, sip a cold one and wait for the perfect set.

🍸 MOCEAN *Bar*

☎ 9300 9888; www.moceanbondi.com;
34a Campbell Pde, Bondi; admission free;
⏲ 6pm-midnight Tue-Sun; 🚌 381 from
Bondi Junction, 380, 389

Sexy surfers and their suntanned girlfriends carve it up to funk and

Paul Jones,
Usher in the Giotto Room, National Gallery

How's the surf this morning? Not really happening – a bit windy. The water's warm though, so it's still good for a swim. **Favourite surf spots?** Bronte and Tamarama. MacKenzies when it's working. Bondi is usually crowded. Maroubra gets crowded too, and everyone's a good surfer there, so it's harder to get waves. **What sort of breaks?** Mostly sandbars; a couple of reefs. The Northern Beaches have a few point breaks. **Is there a 'locals only' culture around here?** Only really at Maroubra. If you were looking for trouble, you'd find out about the locals pretty quickly! **How have the 2005 Cronulla riots affected the vibe?** All-in-all the Eastern Beaches are pretty peaceful. I think everyone learned something from Cronulla – things can get ugly – so they don't push it. **Ever seen a shark?** No. I got out once, but it turned out to be a whale! I've seen dolphins quite a few times.

SYDNEY ROCK POOLS

Sydneysiders aren't always desperate to hurl themselves into the Pacific. Sometimes they just want to swim a few salty laps without malicious dumpers or ocean dwellers to contend with. So inclined, they head for the protected tidal pools built below the cliffs at rocky beach-ends. From north to south, the following beaches have rock pools: Palm, Whale, Bilgola, Newport, Mona Vale, Collaroy, Dee Why, Curl Curl, Freshwater, Queenscliff, Bondi, Bronte, Coogee and Cronulla. Great for kids, they're regularly drained and scoured clean of oysters, sand and seaweed, and except for Bondi Icebergs, they're free.

R&B at this subterranean Bondi bar. The cool, moody interior makes an urbane departure from the sandy stresses of the beach.

 PLAY

☆ BONDI OPEN AIR CINEMA
Cinema
☎ 9209 4614; www.bondiopenair.com
.au; Bondi Pavilion, Queen Elizabeth Dr,
Bondi; tickets $20/18; ☾ 7pm Jan-Feb;
🚌 381 from Bondi Junction, 380, 389;
♿ 👶
The best Sydney can offer: outdoor summer cinema on a massive screen with surround-sound, beachy sunsets and swanky food and wine. In the city, **Open Air Cinema** (☎ 1300 366 649; www.stgeorge
.com.au/openair; Mrs Macquaries Pt, Royal Botanic Gardens; tickets $23/21; ☾ 6.30pm;
🚌 🚌 🚢 Circular Quay) is the same but different. Bookings essential.

☆ DIVE CENTRE BONDI *Activity*
☎ 9369 3855; www.divebondi.com.au;
192 Bondi Rd, Bondi; courses from $195;

☾ 8.30am-6pm Mon-Fri, 7.30am-6pm Sat & Sun; 🚌 381 from Bondi Junction, 380, 389
With so much water around Sydney, it's tempting to see what's under the surface. This reputable company runs lean-to-dive courses and shore and boat dives for absolute beginners through to experienced submariners. Dive sites include North Bondi, Gordons Bay and South Head.

☆ LET'S GO SURFING *Activity*
☎ 9365 1800; www.letsgosurfing.com
.au; 128 Ramsgate Ave, North Bondi; 2hr lesson $85/75, board & wetsuit hire (no instruction) per 2hr $30; ☾ 9am-7pm;
🚌 381 from Bondi Junction, 380, 389
Always wanted to join the rubbery tribe bobbing around in the Bondi waves? Here's your chance: two-hour, small-group lessons including board and wetsuit – paddle out the back, wait for a fat set and get radical, dude. Ask about lessons at Maroubra.

>MANLY

Laid-back Manly clings to a narrow isthmus between ocean and harbour beaches near North Head, Sydney Harbour's northern gatepost. Surrounded by stuffy harbour enclaves, Manly, with it's shaggy surfers, dusty labourers and relaxed locals, makes a refreshing change.

One of the highlights of the Manly experience is actually getting there. The ferry ride from Circular Quay (on either a bumbly, old-time ferry or slick, high-speed JetCat) takes you out towards the heads, weaving through harbour traffic, past ritzy waterside homes and leafy patches of Sydney Harbour National Park – as good as any harbour tour for the price of a ferry ticket.

The Corso connects Manly's ocean and harbour beaches – surf shops, burger joints, juice bars and lousy cappuccino cafés proliferate. The refurbished Manly Wharf has classier cafés, pubs and restaurants, while Sydney Rd has a weekend craft market. The amazingly varied 10km Manly Scenic Walkway (p142) tracks west from Manly around the harbour.

MANLY

⊙ SEE
Manly Art Gallery &
  Museum 1 A2
Manly Quarantine
  Station.......................2 B6
North Fort 3 C6
Oceanworld 4 A3

🛍 SHOP
Mambo 5 B2

🍴 EAT
Bower Restaurant 6 C3
Le Kiosk 7 D3

▶ DRINK
Manly Wharf Hotel.........**8** A3

★ PLAY
Manly Blades..................9 B2
Manly Surf School 10 B1

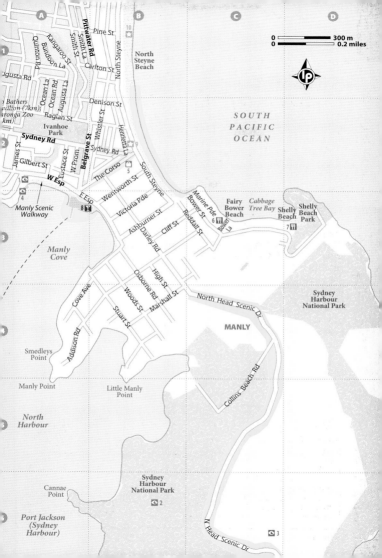

NEIGHBOURHOODS

MANLY

 SEE

MANLY ART GALLERY & MUSEUM

☎ 9976 1420; www.manly.nsw.gov.au/gallery.html; West Esplanade; $3.60/1.20; 🕙 10am-5pm Tue-Sun; ⛴ Manly; 🚍 151, 169 E69 from Wynyard; ♿

A short stroll from Manly Wharf is this passionately managed community gallery, maintaining a local focus with exhibits of surf craft, swimwear and beachy bits-and-pieces. There's also a ceramics gallery, and lots of old Manly photos to peer at.

MANLY QUARANTINE STATION

☎ 9399 3931, 1300 886 875; www.q-station.com.au; North Head Scenic Dr; tours from $25/19; 🚍 135

The eerie Manly Quarantine Station was used to isolate newly arrived epidemic disease carriers between 1832 and 1984. Take a day tour, or rattle some skeletons on the adults-only or family ghost tours. Call ahead for the tour schedule.

NORTH FORT

☎ 9976 6102; www.northfort.org.au; North Head Scenic Dr; $11/8; 🕙 11am-4pm Wed, Sat & Sun; 🚍 135

North Head Scenic Dr, heading south from Manly, provides stunning ocean, harbour and city views. Along the way is the Royal Australian Artillery National Museum at North Fort – tunnels, guns and history for the military-minded.

OCEANWORLD

☎ 8251 7879; www.oceanworld.com.au; West Esplanade; admission $18/13; 🕙 10am-5.30pm, last admission

---

WORTH THE TRIP

A 12-minute ferry ride from Circular Quay or a short drive from Manly, **Taronga Zoo** (☎ 9969 2777; www.zoo.nsw.gov.au; Bradleys Head Rd, Mosman; admission $32/23, Zoo-Pass incl return ferry from Circular Quay, admission & Sky Safari $39/34; 🕙 9am-5pm, last admission 4.30pm; ⛴ from Circular Quay 🚍 247 from Wynyard; ♿) has 75 hectares of bushy harbour hillside chock-full of kangaroos, koalas and similarly hirsute Australians. The zoo's 4000 critters have million-dollar harbour views but seem blissfully unaware of the privilege.

Highlights include the Sky Safari cable car, platypus habitat, Asian elephants display and the nightly **Roar & Snore** (☎ 9978 4791; tickets 132 849; tickets $165/110), an overnight family experience with a night-time safari, barbecue and tents under the stars. Shows and feedings happen throughout the day; there are twilight concerts in summer.

Get up close and personal with creatures of the sea at Oceanworld

4.45pm; Manly 🚌 151, 169 E69 from Wynyard

This ain't the place to come if you're on your way to Manly Beach for a surf. Inside this daggy-looking '80s building are underwater glass tubes through which you become alarmingly intimate with 10ft sharks. Reckon they're not hungry? Shark Dive Xtreme (introductory/certified $245/180) takes you into their world…

🛍 SHOP

📷 MAMBO *Fashion*

☎ 9977 9171; www.mambo.com.au; 80 The Corso; 🕙 10am-6pm; 🚢 Manly 🚌 151, 169 E69 from Wynyard

It's hard to go anywhere in Australia these days without copping an eyeful of Mambo's kooky, bulbous, provocative designs, emblazoned across T-shirts, surfboards, baseball caps, board-shorts and bikinis. Ugly never looked so pretty.

NEIGHBOURHOODS

MANLY

V

WORTH THE TRIP

Romantic Spanish mission–style architecture, sweeping harbour views and outstanding food collide at one of Sydney's enduringly popular restaurants, Balmoral's **Bathers' Pavilion** (☎ 9969 5050; www.batherspavilion.com.au; 4 The Esplanade, Balmoral; ⏲ noon-2.30pm & 6-10.30pm Mon-Fri, 11.30am-2.30pm & 6-10.30pm Sat & Sun; 🚌 175 then 275 from Spit Junction; ♿ 🔽). Under the same roof, Bathers' Café also opens for breakfast from 7am, serving equally scrumptious fare at more democratic prices.

EAT

🍴 BOWER RESTAURANT

Mod Oz $$

☎ /fax 9977 5451; cnr Marine Pde & Bower La; ⏲ 8am-3pm; 🚶 Manly 🚌 151, 169 E69 from Wynyard

Follow the path east from Manly's ocean beach to this little white food room, within sea-spray's reach of Fairy Bower Beach. The 'Big Bower Breakfast' is a knockout, the mains are delicious, it's BYO and they're not afraid to let Olivia Newton John wail from the stereo.

🍴 LE KIOSK *Mod Oz* $$$

☎ 9977 4122; www.lekiosk.com.au; 1 Marine Pde, Shelly Beach; ⏲ noon-3pm daily, 6.30-9.30pm Fri-Sun; 🚶 Manly 🚌 151, 169 E69 from Wynyard; 🔽 ♿

'Le Kiosk' sounds ugly but defines romance – a sandstone cottage, subtle lighting, open fireplace and the lull of lapping waves. The food proves a worthy paramour; swoon over snapper fillet with sautéed calamari, bacon, chilli and cauliflower.

DRINK

🍸 MANLY WHARF HOTEL *Pub*

☎ 9977 1266; www.manlywharfhotel .com.au; Manly Wharf, East Esplanade; admission free; ⏲ 11.30am-midnight Mon-Sat, 11am-10pm Sun; 🚶 Manly Wharf 🚌 151, 169 E69 from Wynyard; ♿

On the harbour side of Manly, the fabulously well-designed Manly Wharf Hotel is perfect for sunny afternoon beers. Tuck away a few middys after a hard day in the surf then pour yourself onto the ferry.

PLAY

⭐ MANLY BLADES *Activity*

☎ 9976 3780; www.manlyblades.com .au; 2/49 North Steyne; hire per hr with safety gear $15, lessons per hr $50; ⏲ 9am-6pm; 🚶 Manly 🚌 151,169 E69 from Wynyard

Work up an appetite or work off your lunch with a skate along Manly Beach promenade. These guys will get you gliding on

Surfboards line up, ready to hit the waves at Manly Beach

ENTER SANDMEN

Manly was one of the first places in Australia to be given a European moniker — history suggests Captain Phillip named the beach after the 'manly' physiques of the Aborigines he met on the sand here in 1788. Perpetuating this reputation today are the bronzed bodysurfing battalions in the waves. If you're feeling inadequate, head for protected Shelly Beach, east of the main beach.

top-of-the-range inline skates, skateboards and mountain bikes. Private skate lessons are available if you're less than proficient.

⭐ MANLY SURF SCHOOL
Activity

☎ 9977 6977; www.manlysurfschool.com; North Steyne Surf Club; lessons per hr incl board & wetsuit $55/45; ⏱ 9am-6pm; 🚢 Manly 🚌 151, 169 E69 from Wynyard

If Bondi isn't your scene, this outfit offers small-group surfing lessons in the Manly shore-breaks. Reformed professional surfers will have you upright on big stable surfboards before you can say, 'Dude, this green room is gnarly!' Also located at Palm Beach and Collaroy.

>WALKING TOURS

Weave your way along the Bendi to Coogee Cliffton Trail

BONDI TO COOGEE CLIFFTOP TRAIL

A quintessential Sydney encounter, this stunning coastal walk rambles south from Bondi Beach along the clifftops to Coogee via Clovelly, Tamarama and Bronte beaches, interweaving panoramic views, swimming spots and foody delights.

Start your explorations at the Eora **Aboriginal rock engravings (1)** between the tower and the cliffs at Bondi Beach Golf Club. Some decades ago they were bizarrely 're-grooved' by the well-meaning but insensitive local council. March south along Military Rd, left into Ramsgate Ave and feel the sea-spray on your skin at the **lookout (2)**. The trail then runs along the rocks to the beach – if the surf's humongous, stay high and dry on Ramsgate Ave. Dunk yourself in the surf then rummage through Sunday's funky **Bondi Markets (3**; p123), or stick your head into **Bondi Pavilion (4**; p123) for an exhibition or performance.

Grab a bite, a bikini or some surfboard wax on **Campbell Parade (5)** then promenade along the beach to Notts Ave and the glistening **Bondi Icebergs (6**; p126) pool and restaurant. Step onto the cliff path at the end of Notts Ave – the blustery sandstone cliffs and grinding Pacific Ocean couldn't be more spectacular (watch for dolphins, whales and surfers). Slide past sex-pot **Tamarama Beach (7**; p15) to **Bronte Beach (8**; p122) – take your pick of beachy cafés for a coffee, a chunky lunch or a quick snack.

Continue past the **Bronte Baths (9)** through the sun-bleached **Waverley Cemetery (10)** where writer Henry Lawson and cricketer Victor Trumper are among the subterranean. Duck into the sunbaked **Clovelly Bowling Club (11)** for a beer or a game of bowls, then breeze past the cockatoos, banksias and canoodling lovers in Burrows Park and Bundock Park to **Clovelly Beach (12**; p15). The concrete terrace skirting the long, skinny bay makes it more a pool than a beach, but the swell still surges in. A beloved friendly grouper fish lived here for many years until he was speared by a tourist. Bring your snorkel, but don't go killing anything.

Follow the footpath up through the car park, along Cliffbrook Pde then down the steps to the upturned dinghies lining **Gordons Bay (13)**. The trail continues through Dunningham Reserve to **Giles Baths (14)**, then lands you smack-bang on glorious **Coogee Beach** (**15**; p122). Swagger into the **Coogee Bay Hotel** (**16**; p129) and toast your efforts with a nice cold lager.

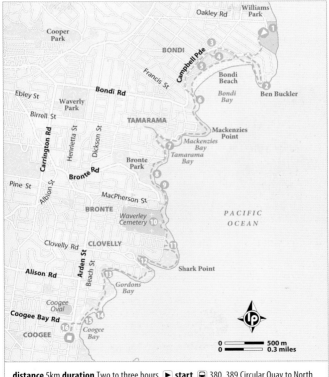

distance 5km **duration** Two to three hours ▶ **start** 🚌 380, 389 Circular Quay to North Bondi ● **end** 🚌 372-4, 313-4 Coogee to Circular Quay

MANLY SCENIC WALKWAY

This epic walk tracks west from Manly through rugged Sydney Harbour National Park (wear strong shoes). It's easy to forget you're right in the middle of Sydney!

Check the surf at **Manly Beach** (**1**) then cruise down The Corso to **Oceanworld** (**2**; p134) on West Esplanade. Scan the view through The Heads from **Fairlight** (**3**), and the yachts tugging on their moorings near **Forty Baskets Beach** (**4**). Kookaburras cackle as you enter **Sydney Harbour National Park** (**5**) and approach **Reef Beach** (**6**). The track becomes steep, sandy and rocky further into the park – keep an eye out for wildflowers, fat goannas sunning themselves and spiders in bottlebrush trees. The views from **Dobroyd Head** (**7**) are unforgettable. Check out the **deserted 1930s sea shanties** (**8**) at the base of Crater Cove cliff, and **Aboriginal rock carvings** (**9**) on an unsigned ledge left of the track before the turnoff to **Grotto Point Lighthouse** (**10**). Becalmed **Castle Rock Beach** (**11**) is at the western end of the National Park.

There are no eateries en route, so eat at Manly beforehand, or picnic on **Clontarf Beach** (**12**). Bus into town from the southern end of **The Spit Bridge** (**13**).

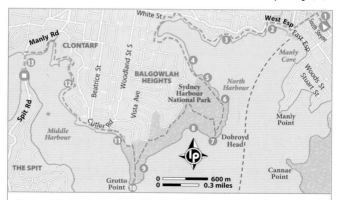

distance 10km **duration** Four hours ▶ **start** 🚢 Circular Quay to Manly 🚌 151 from QVB, 169, E69 from Wynyard ● **end** 🚌 151,169, E69 from The Spit Bridge to Wynyard

SOUTH HEAD SHUFFLE

Take the Watsons Bay ferry from Circular Quay. The **Tree of Knowledge** (1) grew near the pier – an enormous fig where nefarious sea-dogs once convened. Fuel-up on fish and chips at **Doyles on the Beach** (2; p128).

Check out the restored Cove St **fishermen's cottages** (3), then cross Camp Cove Reserve beneath an **ancient fig** (4). From Camp St, turn right into Pacific St then descend the car park steps for magical **harbour views** (5). A **WWII antitorpedo boom** (6) stretched from here to the north shore.

In 1788 Governor Philip landed at **Camp Cove** (7). Take the steps beyond the beach past an 1872 **canon** (8) and gay/nude **Lady Bay** (9). Veer left to the 1858 **Lightkeeper's Cottage** (10), circumnavigating South Head for **North Head views** (11), the red-and-white **Hornby Light** (12) and South Head's original **fortifications** (13), defending Sydney against threats real and imagined. Backtrack through bottlebrush birdlife to Camp Cove.

Trundle along Cliff St to **The Gap** (14), where wedding proposals and suicides abound. The Birrabirragal people once lived at **Gap Bluff** (15). To the right is the **anchor of the Dunbar** (16), wrecked offshore in 1857.

Continue south along the clifftops, or cross **Robertson Park** (17) to the ferry.

distance 2.5km **duration** Two hours
▶ **start** 🚢 Wharf 4, Circular Quay to Watsons Bay ● **end** 🚢 Watsons Bay to Circular Quay

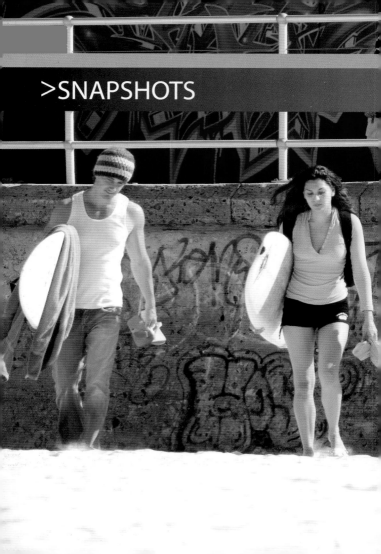

>SNAPSHOTS

Sydney is a worldly, open-minded kinda town, with all sorts of people from all over the place. Shop, sleep, eat, drink and play however you want to – no-one's going to judge you! Perhaps the only rule is to at least look at a beach – they're the best in the world!

Get amongst the locals at Bondi Beach (p122)

ACCOMMODATION

You'll have no problem finding a place to lay your head in Sydney, with solid options in every price range. During the busy summer months, most hotels and hostels increase room rates and cancel promotional deals. Conversely, when tumbleweeds blow through lobbies in the slower winter months, you can often strike a bargain.

For a standard double room in a deluxe hotel, expect to pay $350 and up. For a top-end room you'll pay between $250 and $350. For a standard mid-ranger it'll be $125 to $250, and for a budget double you'll pay up to $125 per night. Midrange to deluxe hotels publish 'rack' rates (standard rates) but it's worth ringing ahead to see if there are any current specials. Many hotels cater primarily to business travellers, so their weekend rates may be lower. Breakfast and onsite parking is sometimes included in the room price. All accommodation has a 10% goods and services tax (GST) included in the price.

Predictably, a view can play a big part in determining the price of a Sydney room. You can almost feel your wallet losing weight as you ride hotel elevators upwards to lofty suites, where Sydney's waterscapes reveal themselves from sky-high balconies. Down at the beach it's the same story – Manly, Bondi and Coogee have plenty of accommodation with surf-strewn views, but you'll be shelling out the dollars for even a glimpse. Between November and February, prices at beachside hotels can be as much as 40% higher. But what the hell, you're on holiday! Why not enjoy yourself?

If you're bunking down in budget lodgings, Sydney has plenty of hostels, heritage pubs and guesthouses. Facilities range from basic dorms to well-kept rooms with en suite, TV and shared kitchens.

Serviced apartments, which offer hotel-style convenience plus self-

haystack.lonelyplanet.com

Need a place to stay? Find and book it at lonelyplanet .com. Over 60 properties are featured for Sydney – each personally visited, thoroughly reviewed and happily recommended by a Lonely Planet author. From hostels to high-end hotels, we've hunted out the places that will bring you unique and special experiences. Read independent reviews by authors and other travellers, and get practical information including amenities, maps and photos. Then reserve your room simply and securely via Haystack – our online booking service. It's all at lonelyplanet.com/accommodation.

catering cooking facilities, can be good value, especially for families. They vary in size from hotel rooms with a bar fridge and microwave to full-blown three-bedroom apartments.

Read up on Sydney's neighbourhoods (p30) before deciding where to settle: party people should head for Kings Cross, Darlinghurst, Paddington or Bondi; shoppers, gourmands and highlight hunters should shoot for The Rocks, city centre, Darling Harbour or Chinatown. If you want to keep things a little more low-key, try Glebe, Potts Point, Surry Hills or Manly. On a short trip, don't be tempted by cheaper rates further out of town – Sydney's public transport is good, but not that good. You don't want to spend most of your time sardined into a train or bus.

WEB RESOURCES

Booking through an accommodation agency like **Tourism NSW** (www.visitnsw .com.au) can sometimes land you a discount. Well worth checking is Lonely Planet's 'Haystack' online accommodation review and booking service (see opposite). For tasty deals on mainstream hotels and serviced apartments try www.check-in.com.au, and of course the big-name players like www .expedia.com.au, www.lastminute.com.au and www.wotif.com.

BEST ON A BUDGET
> Hotel Altamont (www.altamont .com.au)
> Pensione Hotel (www.pensione.com.au)
> Wake Up! (www.wakeup.com.au)
> Woodduck Harbour City Backpackers (www.harbourcitybackpackers.com.au)
> Manly Beach House (www.manly beachhouse.com.au)

BEST FOR SWEET SEDUCTION
> Medusa (www.medusa.com.au)
> Observatory Hotel (www.observatory hotel.com.au)
> Kirketon Hotel (www.kirketon.com.au)
> Hilton (www.sydney.hilton.com)
> Establishment (www.establishment hotel.com)

BEST BANG FOR YOUR BUCK
> Vulcan Hotel (www.vulcanhotel .com.au)
> Hotel 59 (www.hotel59.com.au)
> Blacket (www.theblacket.com)
> Royal Sovereign Hotel (www.royalsov .com.au)
> Y Hotel (www.yhotel.com.au)

BEST BY THE BEACH
> Dive (www.divehotel.com.au)
> Ravesi's (www.ravesis.com.au)
> 101 Addison Rd (www.bb-manly.com)
> Bondi Beach B&B (www.bondibeach -bnb.com.au)
> Manly Pacific (www.accorhotels .com.au)

SNAPSHOTS

GAY & LESBIAN SYDNEY

Gay and lesbian culture is mainstream in Sydney; Oxford St around Taylor Square is the centre of arguably the second-largest gay community in the world. Some local gays think Taylor Sq has become something of a touristy gay ghetto and have migrated to areas of Kings Cross instead. Newtown is home to the city's lesbian scene.

Of course, the highlight of the Sydney gay and lesbian calendar is the annual Mardi Gras festival (p20). Started in 1978 as a political march to commemorate New York's Stonewall riots, Mardi Gras has evolved into a month-long arts extravaganza attracting more visitors and bringing in more tourist dollars than any other event in Australia.

The festival culminates in a raucous street parade and party on the last Saturday in February. The parade – a rampant procession of up to 200 glitzy floats – begins on the corner of Elizabeth and Liverpool Sts at around 7.30pm, and prances the length of Oxford St before trundling down Flinders St, Moore Park Rd and Driver Ave to the Entertainment Quarter. If you want to be among the hundreds of thousands of folks watching the parade, find some friends with a balcony view of Oxford St or cordon off a patch of pavement several hours before it starts. Be sure to bring a milk crate to stand on (oh-so-suddenly scarce) and take some water with you. Tickets to the bacchanalian Mardi Gras Party normally sell out by mid-January and are usually only available to Mardi Gras members, though interstate and overseas visitors can get temporary membership.

The free gay press includes *SX* and *Sydney Star Observer*. *Lesbians on the Loose* (www.lotl.com) also has extensive listings. For counselling and referral call the **Gay and Lesbian Counselling Service of NSW** (☎ 8594 9596; www .glcsnsw.org.au). **Gay & Lesbian Tourism Australia** (www.galta.com.au) has a wealth of information about gay and lesbian travel in Oz.

In NSW it's legal for men to have sex with men over 18, and for women to have sex with women over 16. Despite broad acceptance, there is still a homophobic streak among some community sections and violence against homosexuals is not unknown.

BEST GAY CLUBS
> Arq (p107)
> Phoenix, at Exchange Hotel (p107)
> Slide (p108)
> Midnight Shift (p108)
> Stonewall Hotel (p109)

BEST G&L PUBS, BARS & DRAG
> Imperial Hotel (p86)
> Newtown Hotel (p85)
> Oxford Hotel (p105)
> Sol's Deck Bar (p106)
> Sydney By Diva (p109)

HEALTH & FITNESS

Sydney's sunshine, parks and unashamed vanity provide plenty of impetus to get your pulse pumping and your bod buffed. Most large hotels have a gym and swimming pool for guests; many make these facilities available to visitors for a fee. Otherwise, there's an abundance of independent gyms around town.

Feel like a run? The foreshore from Circular Quay to Woolloomooloo – through the Royal Botanic Gardens to The Domain – is well trodden. Centennial Park, Bondi and Manly beach promenades and the Bondi to Coogee Clifftop Trail (p140) pass beneath many a sweaty sneaker.

With steep hills, narrow streets and traffic, Sydney isn't exactly bicycle-friendly, although some roads do have designated cycle lanes. **Bicycle NSW** (☎ 9281 4099; www.bicyclensw.org.au) publishes *Cycling Around Sydney* detailing city routes and paths. Centennial Park is popular for pedalling – less traffic and long pathways.

It's just plain wrong to come to Sydney and not at least have a swim at the beach. Harbour beaches offer sheltered and shark-netted swimming, but nothing beats (or cures a hangover faster than) a romp in the Pacific Ocean waves. There are 100-plus public swimming pools in Sydney and many beaches have protected rock pools (p131).

If you're itching for a surf, on the south shore get tubed at Bondi, Tamarama, Coogee, Maroubra and Bronte. On the north shore there are a dozen gnarly surf beaches between Manly and Palm Beach. Surfboards, boogie-boards and wetsuits can be hired from seaside shops. For lessons in how to carve up the swell, see Bondi's Let's Go Surfing (p131) and Manly Surf School (p138).

Yoga is so popular here you'd think all of Sydney was looking through its third eye. Bondi Junction is yoga central, with around 10 schools, most teaching both Hatha and Ashtanga yoga. Newtown also has several schools. Check out www.findyoga.com.au to find the nearest school to you.

Sydney's sailing schools are many; a sailing lesson (p75) is a superb way to see the harbour. The **Cruising Yacht Club of Australia** (☎ 9363 9731; www.cyca.com.au) fields general inquiries.

There are hundreds of public tennis courts in Sydney. **Tennis NSW** (☎ 1800 153 040; www.tennisnsw.com.au) lobs up information.

BEST SWIMMING BEACHES
> Camp Cove (p15)
> Shark Bay (p15)
> Clovelly (p15)
> Balmoral (p15)
> Between the flags at Bondi (p122)

BEST SURF BEACHES
> Bronte (p122)
> Tamarama (p15)
> Manly (p132)
> Maroubra (p15)
> Avalon (p15)

SNAPSHOTS

SYDNEY CUISINE

Other Australian cities hate to admit it, but Sydney – with its multicultural melting pot, abundant fresh produce and geographic assets – has won the food trifecta. Adelaide may have the great wines, Melbourne the café culture and Hobart the seafood, but Sydney has it all, and right on Sydney Harbour.

Restaurants hum, and as inner-city gentrification continues, more and more corner pubs are transforming into brasseries, bookshops are installing espresso machines and locals are finding their own kitchens increasingly wearisome.

Modern Australian cuisine – Mod Oz – continues to evolve as chefs consult Asia for fusion ingredients and Europe for technique. Cooking focuses on fresh, healthy eating, drawing on rich and diverse migrant community influences. At the top end, celebrity chefs plate up mini-masterpieces for wealthy corporate crowds. Those on tighter budgets need not despair; thousands of cafés, bistros and restaurants offer innovative, quality meals at moderate prices.

Most of Sydney's licensed restaurants can't serve patrons alcohol unless they order a meal. Many restaurants have a good wine list, pushing Australian product. Restaurant prices are more expensive than in bottle shops – a decent drop will set you back about $30 and up. Wine sold by the glass is also widely available. Many Sydney restaurants advertise themselves as BYO. This means you can Bring Your Own alcohol, though you'll generally be charged a corkage fee ($2 to $5 per bottle, sometimes per person). Some licensed places also allow you to BYO, often restricted to bottled wine only. Smoking is banned in all restaurants, cafés and in the dining areas of pubs and bars.

Cafés and restaurants are generally open seven days, with many cafés serving food from 7am to 10pm. Most restaurants are open for lunch and dinner, closing typically between 3pm and 6pm, while cafés and patisseries are the best bet for breakfast. Bookings are required at the more expensive restaurants, especially for dinner.

A 10% tip is customary for good restaurant service in Sydney, but feel free to vary the amount depending on your satisfaction reaction.

BEST CLASSY BUSINESS EATS
> Aria (p55)
> Forty One (p42)
> Prime (p43)
> Bécasse (p42)
> Bistro Moncur (p118)

MOST TO-DIE-FOR VIEWS
> North Bondi Italian Food (p128)
> Altitude (p55)
> Bondi Icebergs (p126)
> Barzura (p126)
> Aqua Dining (boxed text, p55)

BEST VEGETARIAN
> Bodhi (p42)
> Green Gourmet (p81)
> Mother Chu's Vegetarian Kitchen (p43)
> Zaaffran (p73)
> Chinta Ria, Temple of Love (p72)

BEST SEAFOOD
> Boathouse on Blackwattle Bay (p81)
> Mohr Fish (p94)
> Mongers (p128)
> Doyles on the Beach (boxed text, p128)
> Bungalow 8 (p71)

Opposite Seafood is prepared with love at the Boat on Blackwattle Bay **Above** Bondi Icebergs enjoys a sweeping view

DRINKING

Pubs play a crucial role in Sydney's social scene, ranging from traditional, elaborate 19th-century affairs with pressed tin ceilings, to cavernous, tiled Art Deco masterpieces and mod, minimalist booze rooms. Bars are the domain of Sydney's urbane drinkers, and often have a dress code (oh-so-smart casual).

There are some rambling old pubs in The Rocks, but determining just how old they are is an inexact science. For sassier surrounds and long cocktail lists, join the after-work booze hounds in the city centre and around Circular Quay.

Twenty-four-hour party people head for Darlinghurst and Kings Cross – the trashy main drag, Darlinghurst Rd, has plenty of drinking (and stripping) options, though there are some stylish speakeasies around here too. Glitzy fashionistas populate Paddington's pubs; students and artists drink in Surry Hills. The inner west is great for a low-key schooner – Balmain, Glebe and Newtown have plenty of decent boozers.

Admission to most bars and pubs is free; check www.sydneypubguide.net, www.sydneycafes.com.au/bars.html and www.cheapdrinks.com.au for listings.

Sydney's coffee drinkers are increasingly choosy about where and how they sip their coffee. Caffeine strips include Darlinghurst Rd and Victoria St in Darlinghurst, King St in Newtown and Glebe Point Rd in Glebe.

BEST LOCAL PUBS
> Cricketers Arms Hotel (p94)
> Australian Hotel (p58)
> London Hotel (boxed text, p85)
> Green Park Hotel (p104)
> Lord Nelson Brewery Hotel (p59)

BEST DESIGNER DRINKING DENS
> Ruby Rabbit (p106)
> Zeta (p45)
> Victoria Room (p106)
> Opera Bar (p59)
> Jimmy Lik's (p104)

BEST BREW WITH A VIEW
> Bondi Social (p127)
> Blu Horizon (p58)
> Orbit Bar (p44)
> Loft (p74)
> Manly Wharf Hotel (p136)

BEST COFFEE SHOPS
> Campos (p81)
> Bar Coluzzi (p101)
> Old Fish Shop Café (p83)
> Badde Manors (p81)
> Perry Lane Café (p120)

GALLERY SCENE

Galleries are pivotal in Sydney's visual arts scene, fostering a tense, competitive vibe between them, particularly between the Paddington/Woollahra galleries and their Surry Hills/Redfern competitors. See the Metro section in Friday's *Sydney Morning Herald* and the monthly *Art Almanac* magazine for listings. Many galleries close through Christmas/January and on Mondays; most of them are free.

Over the past 25 years, Australian indigenous art has soared to global heights, a lofty position cemented with the opening of the Musee du quai Branly in Paris in mid-2006. The museum's façade, walls and ceilings have been gloriously painted by Aboriginal artists. Traditional methods and spiritual significance are fastidiously maintained in Aboriginal art, often finding a counterpart in Western materials – the results can be wildly original interpretations of traditional stories and ceremonial designs. Most traditional and contemporary indigenous art available in Sydney's galleries and shops comes from elsewhere in Australia, costing anywhere from $20 to $10,000.

Sydney's city centre and The Rocks are full of cheap-and-nasty tourist shops hocking varnished boomerangs and mass-produced didgeridoos, shimmering under fluoro lights. Avoid them. To ensure you make an informed, authentic purchase and don't perpetuate the nonindigenous cash-in on Aboriginal art's popularity, buy from an authentic dealer selling original art, and if the gallery doesn't pay their artists up-front, ask exactly how much of your money will make it back to the artist or community. Another good test is to request some biographical info on the artists – if the gallery can't produce it, keep walking.

BEST SMALL GALLERIES
> Object Gallery (p90)
> Sherman Galleries (p113)
> Watters Gallery (p37)
> Australian Centre for Photography (p112)
> SH Ervin Gallery (p51)

BEST INDIGENOUS GALLERIES
> Yiribana Gallery, Art Gallery of NSW (p34)
> Hogarth Galleries (p112)
> Artery (p97)
> Original & Authentic Aboriginal Art (p51)
> Gannon House (p50)

SNAPSHOTS

PARKS, WILDLIFE & THE GREAT OUTDOORS

When the galleries, shops and restaurants start to close in, Sydney offers a smorgasbord of outdoorsy possibilities – the sun is shining, the beaches are spacey, and parks are leafy retreats.

If you're hankering for some greenery in the city, head to Hyde Park (Map p33, B4), the CBD's best lunchtime picnic spot; the Domain (Map p33, D4); or Dawes Point Park (Map p49, D1) under the Sydney Harbour Bridge. Paddington's Centennial Park (Map p111, F4) and Jubilee Park (Map p77, B2) at the end of Glebe Point Rd have boundless space.

Want some fauna with your flora? There are great zoos, aquariums and wildlife parks not far from the CBD, or you can head further out. In the western suburbs, **Featherdale Wildlife Park** (☎ 9622 1644; www.featherdale.com.au) at Doonside houses 2000 native Australians eating, sleeping, shagging and generally being beastly. **Koala Park Sanctuary** (☎ 9484 3141; www.koalapark.com) at West Pennant Hills in the north is a 4.5-hectare sanctuary with koalas, kangaroos, wombats, echidnas, dingoes and native birds. **Waratah Park Earth Sanctuary** (☎ 9986 1788; www.waratahpark.com.au) at Duffys Forest in the north was where iconic '60s Australian TV show *Skippy the Bush Kangaroo* was filmed. It's now a free-range park for kangaroos, bandicoots and potoroos.

Broke? Take your book to the beach. If you're worried about getting your gear off, don't be. Victorian conservatism banned daylight bathing in Sydney until 1903. In 1907, a new law permitted neck-to-knee swimming costumes only. By 1930, hems were on the rise – soon nude was rude no more. These days, Sydney's beaches seethe with as much skin as sand.

See also Walking Tours (p139).

BEST WILDLIFE PARKS
> Taronga Zoo (p134)
> Sydney WildlifeWorld (p69)
> Sydney Aquarium (p68)
> Waratah Park Earth Sanctuary (above)
> Featherdale Wildlife Park (above)

BEST PLACES TO CHILL-OUT ON THE GRASS
> Royal Botanic Gardens (p35)
> Observatory Park (p52)
> Jubilee Park (above)
> Centennial Park (above)
> Hyde Park (above)

SHOPPING & MARKETS

Sydney's brash, ingrained commercial culture goes a long way towards explaining its citizens' passion for shopping. Most locals treat it as recreational activity rather than a necessity, evidenced by the teeming, cash-flapping masses at the city's numerous weekend markets. You can buy everything from gumboots to g-strings in Sydney's shops, but some of the more interesting stuff is in the galleries – Aboriginal art (p155) and cutting-edge crafts in particular.

Shopping in central Sydney can be fun, but hectic. The city centre brims with department stores, boutiques, duty-free shops and outdoor stores – shopping here is about as fast and furious as Australia gets. Much more chilled-out are suburban shopping strips like Oxford St, Paddington, Glebe Point Rd, Glebe and King St, Newtown – long, sinuous swathes of boutiques, cafés and bookshops. Queen St, Woollahra is antique-central.

All stores accept major credit cards. If a store accepts travellers cheques, some valid ID – a driving licence or passport – will probably be required as well. A 10% federal Goods and Services Tax (GST) is automatically included in the price of most things you buy. Visitors to Australia are entitled to a refund of any GST paid on items over $300 from one supplier; see p170 for details.

Bargaining and haggling isn't really part of Australian consumer culture – locals tend to think it's somehow undignified and shop around for the best prices instead – but it may work for you at duty-free stores and markets. Most larger stores will arrange shipment or mailing of bulky or fragile items.

BEST WEEKEND MARKETS
> Glebe Market (p78)
> Paddington Market (p116)
> Bondi Markets (p123)
> Balmain Market (boxed text, p78)
> Paddy's Markets (p70)

BEST FROCK SHOPS
> Wheels & Doll Baby (p100)
> Leona Edmiston (p116)
> Capital L (p100)
> Collette Dinnigan (p114)
> Alannah Hill (p41)

SPECTATOR SPORTS

Sydney loves to watch. Basketball, cricket, football, soccer, rugby, surf lifesaving, tennis and yachting draw crowds of onlookers, keen to glimpse the hard-bodied participants and their silky skills.

From April to November, the Sydney Kings dribble around the Sydney Entertainment Centre (p75) in the **National Basketball League** (NBL; www.nbl.com .au). The Sydney Flames play in the **Women's National Basketball League** (WNBL; www.wnbl.com.au).

From October to March, Paddington's Sydney Cricket Ground (SCG) hosts interstate Pura Cup and international Test and World Series cricket matches; see www.baggygreen.com.au.

The **Australian Football League** (AFL; www.afl.com.au) is unique, skilful and awe-inspiring. From March to September, the Sydney Swans glide across the Sydney Cricket Ground and Telstra Stadium at Homebush.

Soccer is gaining fans, thanks to the 2006 World Cup success of the Australian Socceroos. Sydney FC play in the national **A-League** (www .a-league.com.au).

Sydney *adores* winter's **National Rugby League** (NRL; www.nrl.com.au) comp, transpiring at stadia including Paddington's Aussie Stadium. NSW and Queensland collide annually in the State of Origin series. The Australian Wallabies **rugby union** (www.rugbyunion.com.au) team plays internationals in Sydney periodically.

Australian icons, surf lifesavers compete at summer surf carnivals on Sydney's beaches. Contact **Surf Life Saving NSW** (☎ 9300 4000; www.slsa.asn.au).

January's Adidas International tennis tournament happens at the Sydney International Tennis Centre at Homebush; contact **Tennis NSW** (☎ 9763 7644; www.tennisnsw.com.au).

The 18ft skiff yacht racing season runs from September to March. The **Sydney Flying Squadron** (☎ 9955 8350; www.sydneyflyingsquadron.com.au) conducts viewings. On Boxing Day (26 December) Sydney Harbour hosts the start of the harrowing Sydney to Hobart Yacht Race (p22).

>BACKGROUND

The complexities of Aboriginal culture are at last being recognised

BACKGROUND

HISTORY

Australia can seem to be a long way from anywhere in particular – this isolation made it the last great landmass to be 'discovered' by Europeans. But before Sydney Harbour saw its first billow of British sail, indigenous people inhabited the continent for more than 50,000 years, the world's longest continuous cultural history.

ABORIGINAL ORIGINS

When the British first sailed into Warran (the Aboriginal name for Sydney Harbour) there were an estimated 3000 Aborigines living in the area, and around one million across the continent. The Sydney region is the ancestral home of the Eora people (the Ku-ring-gai, Birrabirragal and Cadi tribes) who possessed an intimate understanding of environmental sustainability, spoke three distinct languages and maintained sophisticated sacred and artistic cultures.

Under colonial rule, Aborigines were stripped of legal rights to their land. In a typically ugly pattern of European colonisation, they were systematically incarcerated, killed or driven away by force; many more succumbed to European diseases.

A legacy of 2000 Aboriginal rock engravings exists in the Sydney area, and many Sydney suburbs have Aboriginal names.

EUROPEAN SETTLEMENT

Portuguese navigators first bumped into Australia in the 16th century, followed by Dutch explorers and the enterprising Englishman (read: pirate) William Dampier. British hunger for new world territory landed Captain James Cook on the east coast in 1770. Cook claimed the continent for England and, in a fit of creative genius, named it New South Wales (NSW).

Sailing home, Joseph Banks (Cook's naturalist) suggested relieving Britain's overcrowded prisons by transporting convicts to the new colony. The British government sparked at the concept – faraway convicts were good convicts.

In 1787 the First Fleet set sail from Portsmouth with 759 convicts aboard. At the helm was Captain Arthur Phillip, deigned to become first governor of NSW. Phillip made landfall at Botany Bay on 26 January 1788

BENNELONG

The volatile, puzzled relations between Bennelong, an Eora Aborigine, and the British are emblematic of much early contact.

In 1789 Governor Phillip kidnapped Bennelong to act as an interpreter and go-between. He initially enjoyed life at Government House, but the following years became a confused parade of escape, recapture, anger and misunderstanding. Bennelong travelled with Phillip to England, returning to Australia after two uncomfortable years and retreating from white contact.

Bennelong Point, where a house was built for him and where the Sydney Opera House now stands, bears his name.

before shunting north to Sydney Cove. He flirted with the name 'Albion' but astutely opted for Sydney (the British Home Secretary, Baron Sydney of Chislehurst, was responsible for the colonies at the time).

COLONIAL EXPANSION

In 1800 there were only three small settlements in the colony: Sydney Cove, Parramatta, and on Norfolk Island, adrift in the Pacific 1500km east of Sydney. The continent's vast interior was largely unknown. Over the next 40 years, Sydney bumbled through near-starvation and rum-fuelled political turmoil, while exploration opened up western NSW to settlers. Sydney town grew steadily, with convict transportation continuing until 1840. Free settlers arrived too, but things didn't boom until the 1850s gold rush put a rocket under the economy. Hefty discoveries near Bathurst and in Victoria had prospectors flooding in from Europe, Asia and North America. Sydney's population doubled in a decade.

THE 20TH CENTURY

On 1 January 1901 NSW became a state of the new Australian nation.

Through WWI and the Great Depression, Australia remained culturally and economically tied to Britain, but after the US defended Australia from the Japanese in WWII, a fraternal shift towards America occurred.

Postwar immigrants from the UK, Ireland and the Mediterranean brought spirit and prosperity to Australia in the 1950s and '60s and Sydney's urban area spread like spilt honey.

The face of Sydney changed again during the Vietnam War, when American GIs swarmed to the city on 'Rest and Recreation'. Kings Cross excelled in providing the kind of belt-level R&R that the troops lusted for.

WORST OF SYDNEY

Some things about Sydney can really get on your goat:
> Wheezy air, aircraft cacophony and harbour pollution
> Attitude – big fish, small pond
> Tacky Australiana shops and colonial cash-ins
> Sunburn – the southern sun bites like a shark
> Party, party, party… Don't you people read books?
> Dangerous rips at the beach – swim between the flags!
> Cockroaches – things that go crunch in the night

The bullish world economy of the 1980s sprouted a forest of bombastic new Sydney skyscrapers, with 1988's controversial celebration of the bicentenary of the British landing ruffling indigenous and pro-republican feathers.

SYDNEY TODAY

An expansive metropolis of over four million folks, Sydney's streets buzz with business conducted in dozens of accents and tongues. Hosting the 2000 Olympic Games thrust Sydney into the global limelight, and the city wasn't shy about stepping onto the stage, the flawless success of the Games infusing confidence and pride. The Olympic ebullience is ancient history, but confidence remains.

Simmering racial tensions exploded into mob violence on Sydney's southern beaches in late 2005 – an ugly development that remains unresolvedly snagged in the city's social conscience.

LIFE AS A SYDNEYSIDER

Sydney is irresistibly multicultural, with a quarter of Sydneysiders born overseas. Before WWII Sydney was predominantly Anglo-Irish, but large postwar migrations from Italy, Greece, Yugoslavia, Lebanon and Turkey enriched the mix. The Chinese first arrived during the 1850s gold rush; Asian migration continued with large numbers of Vietnamese after the Vietnam War. Significant numbers have recently arrived from New Zealand, Thailand, Cambodia and the Philippines. Australians cherish their 'outcasts and immigrants' self-image, and despite some racial tensions, Sydneysiders remain generally tolerant of different religions and backgrounds.

A waning majority of Australians are Christian. The Presbyterian, Methodist and Congregational Union churches merged to form the Uniting Church in 1977, although the Anglican Church remains separate. Australia's Irish and Mediterranean heritage keeps Roman Catholic pews warm. Non-Christian minorities abound – Islam is Australia's second-largest religion, Jewish numbers are steady and Buddhism is increasingly popular. Around 13% of Australians claim agnosticism.

ABORIGINAL SOCIETY

Although nonindigenous Australia is at last recognising the complexities of Aboriginal culture, many are still intolerant of urban Aborigines. Aborigines comprise just 0.6% of Sydney's population, but they're marginalised and often cast as social miscreants. Misunderstandings are common, with constructive solutions to indigenous poverty, criminality and health problems placed in the 'too hard' basket. Inner-city Redfern has a large Koori (indigenous southeastern Australian) population, but the suburb's dilapidated heritage houses are fast being consumed by developers.

ETIQUETTE

The Sydney attitude can be aggressive and in-your-face, but locals are usually friendly and open-minded. Gay and lesbian Sydney is riotously uninhibited. Restaurants and sporting arenas are smoke-free. Mobile phone etiquette is forgiving, but turn yours off during meetings, movies and concerts.

Business conduct is straightforward – astute candour will seal the deal; obsequious smooth-talking (aka 'brown nosing') won't. Much business discussion happens after work at the pub – 'a couple of quieties' (a beer or two) often involves more than just a drink. Business dress is sharp with an allowance for individuality.

SHOCK-JOCK RADIO

Sydney radio listeners worship their Oz Rock, but love having a dose of just-right-of-Genghis-Khan opinion rammed down their ears almost as much. Sydney's celebrity 'Shock Jocks' alienate everyone from lesbians to asylum seekers and dole bludgers. Radio rednecks to listen out for (or avoid) include 'Golden Tonsils' John Laws on 2UE (954AM), outrageously opinionated (even for Sydney) Stan Zemanek, also on 2UE, and king of the Shock Jocks Alan Jones, whose defection from 2UE to arch rival 2GB (873AM) sent tremors of disbelief through radio's corridors of power.

BACKGROUND

THE ARTS

Sun, sand, surf and sin are misleading folly – Sydney is no artistic backwater.
The city can't rival New York or London for artistic quantity, but Sydney
breeds similarly bold and adventurous artistic attitudes. Opening nights,
readings and screenings are firmly entrenched in the social calendar.

ARCHITECTURE

Sydney is predominantly a Victorian city, with much of the city's
expensive inner-city housing dating from this era. Colonial structures
surviving Sydney's wholesale 20th-century development are scarce,
but remnants are culturally celebrated. Classy Art Deco design
reigned between the two world wars, most obviously (and perhaps
incongruously) in Sydney pub architecture. Some unbelievable eyesores
sprouted with the lifting of the 150ft building height limit in the late
1950s, with many architects accused of lazily dominating Sydney's
splendorous natural setting rather than designing anything of objective
or complementary beauty. Jørn Utzon's Sydney Opera House stands as a
beacon of architectural delight as the CBD continues its rise.

DANCE

Dance and Sydney's body-focused audiences go hand-in-hand (and cheek-
to-cheek). Australian dancers have a fearless reputation for awesome
physical displays (and sometimes a lack of costume). The talented
Australian Ballet troupe tours a mixed programme of classical and modern
ballets, frocking-up four times a year at the Sydney Opera House.

Graeme Murphy's Sydney Dance Company (p61) leads Australia
in contemporary dance. The acclaimed Bangarra Dance Theatre
(p59) conjures up an incendiary blend of 50,000 years of indigenous
performance tradition and vigorous new choreography.

FILM

Sydney's film industry boomed in the 1990s but things have tailed off
recently, with the government failing to support the film industry with
financial incentives. The best 1990s efforts, such as *Strictly Ballroom*,
Shine, *Muriel's Wedding* and *Priscilla – Queen of the Desert*, consolidated
Sydney's reputation as a top-shelf production location, while local actors
such as Russell Crowe, Nicole Kidman, Naomi Watts, Cate Blanchett and
Geoffrey Rush rode the Hollywood fame train.

SYDNEY ON THE SILVER SCREEN

Sydney sure is a good-lookin' sheila (see Language, p177), a fact not overlooked in these Sydney movies:

> *Two Hands* (1999; director Gregor Jordan) – vicious humour in Sydney's criminal underworld.
> *Looking for Alibrandi* (2000; director Kate Woods) – growing up Italian in Sydney suburbia.
> *Lantana* (2001; director Ray Lawrence) – mystery for grown-ups; a meditation on love, truth and grief.
> *Candy* (2006; director Neil Armfield) – Heath Ledger and Abbie Cornish in drug demise; the film adaptation of Luke Davies' 1998 grunge novel.
> *Bra Boys* (2007; director Sunny Abberton) – Maroubra's bad-boys in stark profile; narrated by the dulcet Russell Crowe.

Sydney's multimillion-dollar Fox Studios has rolled out big-budget world extravaganzas including the *Matrix* trilogy, *Mission Impossible 2*, the *Star Wars* prequels and Sydneysider Baz Luhrmann's *Moulin Rouge*.

Sydney has two international film festivals: Tropfest (p21) and Bondi's Flickerfest (p20).

MUSIC

Wrap your ears around Sydney's sounds: world-class opera, grungy pub bands, funky electronic acts. Local musos gig at pubs and clubs around the city, while international acts rock big venues like the Sydney Entertainment Centre (p75) and the Enmore Theatre (p86).

Sydney's raucous rock scene (the Easybeats, Midnight Oil, Silverchair etc) ailed under '90s noise and licensing restrictions, but is enjoying a rockin' revival. There's an effervescent dance-music scene, with clubs and dance parties catering to every sub-genre. Jazz and blues kick out the jams in venues like the Basement (jazz; p63) and pubs like the Empire (blues; p86).

Opera Australia wails through 18 operas a year, based (appropriately) at the Sydney Opera House (p10). The Sydney Symphony, Australia's biggest orchestra, plays 140 concerts annually, frequently at the Opera House and City Recital Hall (p45).

January's Sydney Festival (p20) tunes Sydney's diverse musical movements. The Sydney Discography (p166) lists some sound Sydney sounds.

SYDNEY DISCOGRAPHY

> *Gossip* (Paul Kelly) – 'Incident on South Dowling', 'Randwick Bells' are ringing, and 'Darlin' It Hurts' to see you down in Darlinghurst tonight.
> *Harry's Café de Wheels* (Peter Blakeley) – The only album ever named after a pie cart. Don't bother listening to it though.
> *Hourly, Daily* (You Am I) – Recorded in Sydney and oozing suburban mid-afternoon sensibility.
> *Love this City* (The Whitlams) – The band's named after Australia's grooviest prime minister, Gough Whitlam; the album digs into Sydney's best and worst.
> *10, 9, 8...* (Midnight Oil) – '*Sydney, nights are warm, daytime telly, blue rinse dawn...*'

LITERATURE

Sydney's literary lineage dates back to the late 1800s, when local writers like Henry Lawson, AB 'Banjo' Patterson and Miles Franklin spiked a vernacular vein. Modern Australian authors like Patrick White (Nobel Prize 1973), Tom Keneally (Booker Prize 1982) and Peter Carey (Booker Prize 1988 and 2001) all spent time in Sydney, and have redefined what being Australian is. Keep an eye out for books by Robert Drewe, Helen Garner, David Malouf, Kate Grenville, Janette Turner Hospital, Thea Astley, Eleanor Dark, Drusilla Modjeska and Amanda Lohrey, all of whom have lived in or dedicated their pages to Sydney.

The vibrant Sydney literary scene peaks every year with the Sydney Writers Festival (p21). See www.austlit.edu.au and for more info.

PAINTING

Like Australian writers prior to the 1880s, Australian painters applied European stylings to the Antipodean condition, failing to capture Australia's bleached light, ragged forests and earthy colours with any certainty. Melbourne's distinctly Australian Heidelberg School changed this in 1885. Tom Roberts and Arthur Streeton brought the Heidelberg techniques to Sydney in 1891.

Expressionists of the 1940s such as Sidney Nolan and Arthur Boyd blazed their way to prominence and rattled the national psyche. Sydney's Brett Whiteley (1939–92) was an internationally notorious *enfant terrible* who let loose with luscious, colourful, orgasmic canvases. His Surry Hills studio is preserved as an interactive art gallery (p90).

ABORIGINAL ART

Art is integral to Aboriginal culture, a conduit between past and present, supernatural and earthly, people and land. Aboriginal art is immersed in 'The Dreaming' – a vast unchanging network of life and land tracing back to spiritual ancestors.

Aboriginal art gained broad cross-cultural exposure in the 1980s and '90s when galleries discovered its virtue and value. Dot paintings are exquisite, as are Tiwi Island woodcarvings and fabrics, Arnhem Land bark paintings and central Australian prints. Many Sydney galleries specialise in Aboriginal and Torres Strait Islander art. See p155 for some tips on how to responsibly approach an indigenous art purchase.

THEATRE

Sydney's theatrical tastes can seem stuck in a 1970s holding pattern – mainstream blockbuster musicals and crowd-friendly productions are the norm, but some small companies stage more experimental works. Australia's geographic isolation and sense of 'cultural cringe' means that truly local productions are rare, and not particularly well paid. Actors tend to migrate towards film and TV, or crack the boards overseas.

Sydney's most successful theatre company is the Sydney Theatre Company (p63). The National Institute of Dramatic Art (NIDA) is a breeding ground for new talent – Cate Blanchett, Judy Davis, Mel Gibson and Hugo Weaving are all graduates. Smaller theatre companies like

BOOKISH SYDNEY

Browse the bookshelves for a Sydney-centric read:

> *The Harp in the South* and *Poor Man's Orange*, Ruth Park (1948 & 1949) – impoverished Surry Hills family life
> *Voss*, Patrick White (1957) – the unforgiving outback versus Sydney's colonial life
> *Unreliable Memoirs*, Clive James (1980) – boy-Clive in Sydney's southern 'burbs
> *The Bodysurfers*, Robert Drewe (1983) – seductive stories from the Northern Beaches
> *Lilian's Story*, Kate Grenville (1985) – the life of Sydney eccentric Bea Miles
> *The Last Magician*, Janette Turner Hospital (1992) – seedy corruption around Newtown Station
> *He Died with a Felafel in His Hand*, John Birmingham (1994) – beer, bongs and cockroaches
> *The Cross*, Mandy Sayer (1995) – sleazy '70s Kings Cross murder
> *30 Days in Sydney*, Peter Carey (2001) – tales from behind the Venetian blinds
> *Safety*, Tegan Bennet (2006) – truth and frailty on the banks of the Parramatta River

Griffin (p109), Company B (p95) and the Darlinghurst Theatre Company (p107) are producing exciting work.

Notable stage actors include Angie Millikin, Jackie Weaver, Marcus Graham and John Howard (no, not the prime minister). Directors of note include John Bell, Neil Armfield, Adam Cook and Lindy Davies.

ENVIRONMENT

Sydney and its stupendous harbour are encircled by parks and forests. Beauty comes naturally, as does the incentive to keep things looking good. Locals generate as much mess as anyone, but they're also environmentally aware.

Sydney's Gods of Rain don't pull any punches, with summer downpours sending people scurrying. Historically, Sydney's harbour and beaches gasped and clogged after heavy rains, but million-dollar litter traps now prevent a lot of rubbish flowing into the harbour. Still, swimming at harbour beaches such as Balmoral or Seven Shillings after a big storm can be a soupy experience.

Airport noise creates headaches under the flight path – the government has tried to calm under-slept locals by spreading aircraft trajectories.

The air in the city and eastern suburbs is generally clean and breezy; the west can get wheezy.

GOVERNMENT & POLITICS

Sydney is the capital of NSW and seat of state government, which holds court in Parliament House on Macquarie St.

NSW has two main political parties: the left-wing Australian Labor Party and right-wing Liberal/National party coalition. At the time of writing, Labor had just been re-elected to government, with Premier

A WHALE OF A TIME

Apocalyptic commercial whaling in the 19th century drove them away, but whales have recently returned to Sydney Harbour. A traditional detour for whales migrating south for the summer, the harbour has hosted pods of humpback and southern right whales breaching below the Harbour Bridge regularly over the past five years. If you're lucky enough to be out on the water with them (p63), give them a wide berth – they're bigger than you are, and humanity owes them a little peace and quiet.

Morris Iemma at the wheel. Members of the Australian Greens, Australian Democrats and several independents also populate Parliament.

Sydneysiders can be wryly cynical about state politics. State elections irritate the public every four years, and there's not a whole lotta love for Iemma's Labor machine that some people feel has abandoned traditional values to court big-business dollars. Your views on Australia's prospective move towards becoming a republic may see you lauded as a visionary, or tarred, feathered and banished to the Blue Mountains.

Don't expect much saucy media coverage of politicians' sex lives. Perhaps it's an aesthetic damnation, but locals don't drool over Clinton-Lewinsky/Tory-sex-romp scandals. A contraceptive distance is maintained between the media and politicians.

ECONOMY

Sydney is Australia's chief commercial, financial and industrial centre, whipping up a quarter of Australia's economic activity. As a financial centre, Sydney houses 'the big three' – the Reserve Bank of Australia, Australian Stock Exchange and Sydney Futures Exchange – and most of Australia's major banks have their head offices in Sydney. It's also a transport epicentre, with two harbours – Port Jackson (Sydney Harbour) and Botany Bay – a hyperactive airport and a spider-web rail network. The majority of Australia's foreign trade flows through Sydney and NSW. Despite all this, Sydney's economic growth rate recently nudged below the 3.7% national average for the first time in years – Premier Morris Iemma is starting to feel the heat!

Sydney tourism is coming down from a boom period, but still employs one in 12 workers. Brisbane and Cairns have taken a slice of Sydney's tourist pie, but expect Sydney to handle your arrival with aplomb.

DIRECTORY

TRANSPORT
ARRIVAL & DEPARTURE

AIR

Sydney's major airport is **Kingsford Smith Airport** (☎ 9667 9111; www .sydneyairport.com.au), 10km south of the city centre. The T1 (international) and T2 and T3 (domestic) terminals are a 4km, $4.50 bus or train ride apart. Getting to the city from Kingsford Smith (or vice versa) is easiest by train or car. To confirm arrival/departure times, call airlines directly or log on to the airport website's 'Flight Search'.

BUS

Interstate and regional bus travellers arrive at **Sydney Coach Terminal** (☎ 9281 9366; fax 9281 0123; cnr Eddy Ave & Pitt St; ☿ 6am-10.30pm), outside Central Station. The major bus companies have offices nearby.

TRAIN

Sydney's main rail terminus for Countrylink interstate and regional services is **Central Station** (☎ 13 22 32; www.countrylink.info; Eddy Ave). Staffed ticket booths are open 6am to 10pm; ticket machines operate 24 hours. Call for information, arrival and departure times and reservations.

VISA

Visas are required for all overseas visitors except New Zealand nationals who sheepishly receive a 'special category' visa on arrival. Visa application forms are available from diplomatic missions, travel agents, the **Department of Immigration and Multicultural Affairs** (☎ 13 18 81; www.immi .gov.au), or visit the **Australian Electronic Travel Authority** (www.eta.immi.gov.au).

CUSTOMS, DUTY FREE & TAX REFUNDS

Cash amounts of more than A$10,000 and goods of animal or

CLIMATE CHANGE & TRAVEL

Travel – especially air travel – is a significant contributor to global climate change. At Lonely Planet, we believe that all travellers have a responsibility to limit their personal impact. As a result, we have teamed with Rough Guides and other concerned industry partners to support Climate Care, which allows travellers to offset the greenhouse gases they are responsible for with contributions to energy-saving projects and other climate-friendly initiatives in the developing world. Lonely Planet offsets all staff and author travel. For more information, turn to the responsible travel pages on www.lonelyplanet.com. For details on offsetting your carbon emissions and a carbon calculator, go to www.climatecare.org.

TRAVEL TO/FROM THE AIRPORT

	Taxi	Train	Bus: Sydney Airporter	Bus: Manly Airport Bus
Pick-up point	Outside domestic & international terminals	Below domestic & international terminals	Outside domestic & international terminals	Outside domestic & international terminals
Drop-off point	Anywhere	Central, Town Hall, Wynyard, Circular Quay, St James and Museum, connecting to any train station	Central Sydney hotels	Manly
Duration	To centre, 30min	To Central station, 15min	To central hotels, 30min	To Manly, 45min–1hr
Cost	To Central station, $25; to Circular Quay, $25-35	To Central station from domestic, terminal single/return $12.50/18; from international terminal $13/18.50	Single/return $12/20	Single/return $30/63
Other		No service midnight–5am, otherwise every 15 minutes; return fares are cheaper after 9am & on weekends	No service 11pm–5am; bookings required	No service 11pm–5am; bookings required
Contact	See p176	Airport Link (☎ 13 15 00; www.airportlink.com.au)	Kingsford Smith Transport (☎ 9666 9988; www.kst.com.au)	☎ 0500 505 800; manlyairportbus@hotmail.com

vegetable origin must be declared at customs. **Australian Customs** (☎ 1300 363 263; www.customs.gov.au) doesn't tolerate smugglers – don't even think about it. Travellers over 18 years can import 2.25L of liquor, 250 cigarettes or 250g of tobacco and dutiable goods up to the value of A$900 per person (A$450 for under 18s).

Australia has a 10% Goods and Services Tax (GST) automatically applied to most purchases, though some food items are exempt. If you purchase goods with a total minimum value of $300

DIRECTORY

from any one supplier within 30 days of departure from Australia, you're entitled to a GST refund. You can get a cheque refund at the designated booth located beyond Customs at Sydney Airport. Contact the **Australian Taxation Office** (☎ 13 28 66, www.ato.gov.au) for details.

GETTING AROUND

Central Sydney is very pedestrian friendly; public transport is the best option for the surrounding suburbs. Trains, buses and ferries run by the **State Transit Authority of NSW** (STA; ☎ 13 15 00; www.131500.com.au) are convenient, reliable and good value. Contact them for information or visit their Circular Quay information booths. Beware: the maximum fare-dodging fine is $550!

In this book, the nearest train/Monorail/Metro Light Rail/ferry station or bus route is noted after the 🚆 Ⓜ 🚋 ⚓ or 🚌 icon in each listing.

RECOMMENDED MODES OF TRANSPORT

	Circular Quay	Bondi Beach	Kings Cross	Manly
Circular Quay	n/a	Bus 40min	Train 15min	JetCat 15min
Bondi Beach	Bus 40min	n/a	Bus to Bondi Junction 15min then train 15min	Bus 40min then JetCat 15min
Kings Cross	Train 15min	Train to Bondi Junction 15min then bus 15min	n/a	Train 15min then JetCat 15min
Manly	JetCat 15min	JetCat 15min then bus 40min	JetCat 15min then train 15min	n/a
Newtown	Train 20min	Train to Bondi Junction 30min then bus 15min	Train 25min	Train 20min then JetCat 20min
Paddington	Bus 20min	Bus 20min	Bus 10min or walk 20min	Bus 20 min then JetCat 15min
Surry Hills	Bus 15min	Bus 30min	Bus 20min	Bus 15min then JetCat 15min
Glebe	Bus 20min	Bus 20min then train to Bondi Junction then bus 15min	Bus 20min then train 15min	Bus 30min then JetCat 15min

TRAVEL PASSES

The good-value **SydneyPass** (☎ 13 15 00; www.sydneypass.info) includes bus, rail and ferry transport, travel on the Sydney and Bondi Explorer buses (see p174), harbour ferry cruises (p61) and a return trip on the Airport Express train (p170). A three-/five-/seven-day Sydney-Pass costs $110/145/165. They're available from the Sydney Visitor Centre (p180) at The Rocks and Darling Harbour, the Circular Quay Bus TransitShop and Sydney Ferries ticket offices, or onboard the Explorer buses.

The STA **DayTripper** (☎ 13 15 00; www.cityrail.info) is a day pass ($15.50) letting you ride most trains, buses and ferries with discounts at an array of attractions. Available from STA ticket outlets.

BUS

Buses run almost everywhere, more slowly than trains. Bondi, Coogee and parts of the North Shore are serviced only by

Newtown	Paddington	Surry Hills	Glebe
Train 20min	Bus 20min	Bus 15min	Bus 20min
Bus to Bondi Junction 15min then train 30min	Bus 20min	Bus 30min	Bus 15min then train to Central then bus 20min
Train 25min	Bus 10min or walk 20min	Bus 20min	Train 15 min to Central then bus 20min
JetCat 15min then train 20min	JetCat 15min then bus 20min	JetCat 15min then bus 15min	JetCat 15min then bus 30min
n/a	Bus 35min	Bus 20min	Bus 15min or walk 20min
Bus 35min	n/a	Bus 10min, or walk 20min	Bus 30min
Bus 20min	Bus 10min or walk 20min	n/a	Walk 10min then bus 20min
Bus 15min or walk 20min	Bus 30min	Bus 20min then walk 10min	n/a

bus. Nightrider buses operate skeletally after regular buses and trains cease around midnight. Call the **Transport Infoline** (☎ 13 15 00; www.131500.com.au), or check the **Sydney Buses** (www.sydneybuses.info) website for details.

The main city bus stops are Circular Quay (Map p49, D3), Wynyard Park on York St (Map p33, A2) and Railway Square (Map pp66–7, D8). Many buses also stop outside the Queen Victoria Building on George and York Sts.

Buy tickets from newsagencies, Bus TransitShops and on buses (having the correct change helps to prevent bus driver wrath). If you buy a prepaid ticket you must validate it by inserting it into the onboard machines near the entrance. Fares start at $1.70; most trips are under $3.50. There are Bus TransitShops on the Alfred/Loftus St corner in Circular Quay (Map p49, D4), near Wynyard Station on Carrington St (Map p33, A2), at Railway Square (Map pp66–7, D8) and outside the Queen Victoria Building on York St (Map p33, A4).

Bus routes starting with an X indicate limited-stop express routes; those with an L have limited stops. Bus routes listed in this book depart from Circular Quay unless otherwise indicated.

If you're taking public transport to Bondi or the Eastern Beaches,

the quickest way is to take the train to Bondi Junction (between Woollahra and Bondi Beach), then jump on a bus.

Special Services

The STA's red **Sydney Explorer** (☎ 13 15 00; www.sydneypass.info/sydneyexplorer) bus follows a two-hour, 27-stop, hop-on, hop-off loop from Circular Quay through Kings Cross, Chinatown, Darling Harbour and

USEFUL BUS ROUTES FROM CIRCULAR QUAY

Place	Route No
Balmain	432-4, 441-2
Bondi Beach	380, 389 from Circular Quay, 381 from Bondi Junction
Coogee	372-4, 313-4 from Circular Quay, 353 from Bondi Junction
Darling Harbour	443, 456
Glebe	431-4
Kings Cross	323-7, 324-5, 333
Leichhardt	413, 435-8, 440
Manly	151, 169, E69 from Wynyard
Maroubra	376-7, 395-6, X77, X96
Newtown	422-3, 426, 428
Paddington	378, 380, 389
Surry Hills	301-4, 308-10, 343, 375, 390-1
Watsons Bay from Bondi Junction	324-5, L24 from Circular Quay, L82

The Rocks, with pithy on-board commentary and discounted entry to attractions. Buses run every 20 minutes from 8.40am to 5.20pm; tickets cost adult/child $39/19 from drivers and Bus TransitShops.

Prices are identical for the blue **Bondi Explorer** (☎ 13 15 00; www.sydneypass.info/bondiexplorer) bus, which does a two-hour, 19-stop loop of the inner city and eastern suburbs, including Paddington, Double Bay, Vaucluse, Watsons Bay and Bondi Beach. Buses run every 30 minutes from 8.45am to 4.15pm.

CitySightseeing Sydney & Bondi Tours (☎ 9567 8400; www.city-sightseeing.com) is a privately run rival/alternative to the Explorer buses, with similar services and prices.

TRAIN

CityRail

Sydney's trains are the deft way to get around town. Trains run from around 5am to midnight. There are 24-hour ticket machines at most stations but humans are usually available too if you'd rather talk to something that'll listen. There's a **CityRail Information Booth** (Map p49, D4; ☎ 13 15 00; www.131500.com.au; ⏰ 9.05am-4.50pm) behind Wharf 5 at Circular Quay. For train routes, see the CityRail map on the pull-out sheet map.

Monorail

The **Metro Monorail** (☎ 9285 5600; www.metromonorail.com.au) is a lugubrious elevated worm circling around Darling Harbour and the city. A circuit costs $4.50; a day pass $9. The Monorail runs every four minutes from 7am to 10pm from Monday to Thursday, to midnight on Friday and Saturday, and from 8am to 10pm Sunday.

Metro Light Rail (MLR)

The future-slick **MLR** (☎ 9285 5600; www.metrolightrail.com.au) glides between Central Station and Pyrmont via Chinatown and Darling Harbour. A single ride costs between $3 and $4; a day pass $8.50. Trains run every 15 minutes from 6am to midnight, every 30 minutes from midnight to 6am. The service beyond Pyrmont to Lilyfield stops at 11pm Sunday to Thursday, midnight Friday and Saturday.

FERRY

Sydney transport's most civilised options – harbour ferries, JetCats (to Manly) and RiverCats (to Parramatta) – depart from Circular Quay. The **Ferry Information Office** (Map p49, D3; ☎ 9207 3170; www.sydneyferries.info; ⏰ 7am-5.45pm Mon-Sat, 8am-5.45pm Sun) handles inquiries. A one-way inner-harbour ferry ride costs around $5; many ferries have connecting bus services.

TAXI

Taxis can be flagged down when their top-light is aglow. There are patrolled Friday/Saturday night taxi ranks around town, including one on Park St between Pitt and Castlereagh Sts, and at Central, Wynyard and Circular Quay stations. A short ride between the city and the inner suburbs will cost around $20; to/from the airport from $25 to $35. Some reliable operators:

Arrow Taxis ☎ 13 22 11
Legion ☎ 13 14 51
Premier Cabs ☎ 13 10 17
Taxis Combined ☎ 8332 8888

CAR & MOTORCYCLE

Masochistic? Bring your car into central Sydney. The city has a confusing spaghettilike one-way street system, parking is hell and parking inspectors are ruthless demons (also from hell). Tow-away zones prevail, and private car parks are expensive – around $15 per hour.

A car is, however, invaluable for exploring outer Sydney. Many hotels include parking in accommodation packages. Red-light and speed cameras are common – rental companies will send you your fines plus hefty 'processing' fees. There's a $3 southbound toll on the Sydney Harbour Bridge and Tunnel; $4 northbound on the Eastern Distributor. Sydney's main motorways are also tolled.

PRACTICALITIES

BUSINESS HOURS

Banks, businesses and stores are closed on public holidays (opposite). Museums and other attractions often close on Christmas Day and Boxing Day. Banks open from 9.30am to 4pm Monday to Thursday, most until 5pm on Friday; some large city branches open from 8am to 6pm Monday to Friday. Post offices open 9am to 5pm Monday to Friday; some open 10am to 2pm on Saturday as well.

Businesses and shops open from 9am to 5pm Monday to Wednesday, Friday and Saturday, with late-night shopping until 9pm on Thursday. Sunday hours are usually 11am to 5pm. Pubs open from 11am to midnight; bars from around 4pm until late. Restaurants open around noon to 3pm for lunch, then close until dinner from 6pm to 10pm; some close on Sunday and/or Monday.

DISCOUNTS

Many attractions offer concession/child/family/senior discounts. In this book concession prices are listed after adult prices (eg $15/7.50).

The **See Sydney & Beyond Card** (☎ 1300 661 711; www.seesydney card.com.au) offers admission to a wide range of Sydney's attractions including sightseeing tours, harbour cruises, museums, historic buildings and wildlife parks. One-/two-/three-/seven-day cards cost $65/119/149/209, available online or at the Sydney Visitor Centre (p180). The two-/three-/seven-day cards are also available with public transport included for $159/205/275.

The Heritage Housing Trust's **Ticket Through Time** (☎ 8239 2288; www .hht.net.au/visit/admission_prices) gets you into all 11 of the HHT's Sydney houses and museums, including Vaucluse House (p123), Government House (p50), Elizabeth Bay House (p97), Justice & Police Museum (p50), Museum of Sydney (p35), Hyde Park Barracks Museum (p35) and Susannah Place (p52). Tickets cost adult/concession/child/family $30/15/15/60; visit four or more sights and you'll save yourself a bit of hard-earned cash.

HOLIDAYS

New Year's Day 1 January
Australia Day 26 January
Good Friday & Easter Monday Late March/early April
Anzac Day 25 April
Queen's Birthday Second Monday in June
Bank Holiday First Monday in August
Labour Day First Monday in October
Christmas Day 25 December
Boxing Day 26 December

INTERNET

Internet cafés proliferate throughout Sydney, or you can jump online at public libraries and many hotels. Expect to pay anywhere between $1.50 and $4.50 per hour. Wireless access is increasingly popular.

Lonelyplanet.com offers speedy links to many of Sydney's websites. Others useful resources include the following:

Best Restaurants (www.bestrestaurants .com.au) Reviews, menus and booking info for the best eats on Sydney's streets.
Bureau of Meteorology (www.bom.gov.au) Should I bring a jacket, or will a T-shirt be OK?
Sydney City Council (www.cityofsydney.nsw .gov.au) All the boring stuff, plus festival and events listings.
Sydney City Guide (www.citysearch.com .au) Harbour town news, arts, eating and entertainment reviews.
Surf Report (www.realsurf.com) Check the swell and get amongst it.

LANGUAGE

If you're not from Australia, you'll find the local lingo (Strine) to be colourful, disarming and bamboozling all at once. Lonely Planet's *Australian Phrasebook* is the definitive guide, but here's a handful of Strine essentials:

arvo afternoon
barbie barbecue
beaut, **bewdy**, **bonza** superb
bloke man
bludger lazy oaf
bugger off depart with haste (earnest instruction)

crack the shits to express utmost irritation
crook ill or substandard
dead horse tomato sauce, ketchup
dead set yes, that's correct
dunny toilet
fair dinkum honest, genuine
flaming galah foolish individual
flat out really busy or fast
footy football (Australian Rules or Rugby League)
g'day hello
hard yakka hard work
taking the piss humorous deception
mate generic informal address
mozzie mosquito
no worries, no wukkin furries everything's under control
see ya goodbye
piss beer
sheila woman
shoot through leave
strewth annoyed exclamation
tinnie aluminium boat or beer can
true blue authentically Australian
tucker food
youse more than one person

MEDICAL SERVICES

Hospitals with 24-hour accident and emergency departments include the following:

Royal Prince Alfred Hospital (Map p77, C4; ☎ 9515 6111; www.cs.nsw.gov.au/rpa; Missenden Rd, Camperdown)

St Vincent's Hospital (Map pp98-9, D7; ☎ 8382 7111; wwwsvh.stvincents.com.au; cnr Victoria & Burton Sts, Darlinghurst)

Sydney Hospital & Sydney Eye Hospital (Map p33, C3; ☎ 9382 7111; www.sesahs .nsw.gov.au/sydhosp; 8 Macquarie St)

MONEY

CURRENCY

The Australian dollar is divided into 100 cents. When paying with cash, prices are rounded up or down to the nearest 5 cents. There are coins for $2, $1, 50¢, 20¢, 10¢ and 5¢; notes for $100 (an 'avocado'), $50 (a 'pineapple'), $20 (a 'lobster'), $10 and $5.

COSTS

Not including accommodation, an average Sydney day with midrange restaurant meals, public transport, sight admission, a taxi ride and a couple of beers at the pub will set you back $150 to $200.

American Express, Diners Club, MasterCard and Visa credit cards are all widely accepted. Travellers cheques are accepted in banks, large hotels and duty-free stores; those in Australian dollars can generally be exchanged at banks without fees. There are 24-hour ATMs at most banks, and some pubs and clubs. Shops and retail outlets have eftpos facilities for on-the-spot debit-card payments.

NEWSPAPERS & MAGAZINES

Daily newspapers include the tabloid *Daily Telegraph* (www .dailytelegraph.news.com.au) and the broadsheets *Sydney Morning*

Herald (www.smh.com.au), the *Australian* (www.theaustralian.news.com.au) and the *Australian Financial Review* (www.afr.com).

Magazines with current affairs articles worth reading include the *Bulletin* (www.bulletin.ninemsn.com.au) and the Australian *Time* (www.time.com). For fashion and design, check out *Vogue Australia* (www.vogue.com.au) and *GQ* (www.vogue.com.au/in_vogue/gq). Australia's *Rolling Stone* (www.rollingstone.com) rocks.

Free street press covering local music and entertainment shenanigans includes *Drum Media* (www.drummedia.com.au), *The Brag* (rock and alternative; www.thebrag.com) and *3D World* (club and dance; www.threedworld.com.au). *This Week in Sydney* is a free tourist mag. Also check out the free nightly tabloid *MX* (www.mxnet.com.au) and the gay and lesbian *SX* (www.evolutionpublishing.com.au).

POST

Stamps are sold at post offices in most suburbs and most newsagencies. It costs 50¢ to send a postcard or standard letter within Australia. Airmail letters (weighing up to 50g) cost $1.20 to the Asia/Pacific region; $1.80 to the rest of the world. Postcards to anywhere outside Australia cost $1.10.

TELEPHONE

Public payphones are either coin- or card-operated; local calls cost 50¢. Many also accept credit cards. Local and international phonecards range in value from $5 to $50 – look for the phonecard logo on display at retail outlets.

Mobile phone numbers have four-digit prefixes beginning with 04. Australia's digital network is compatible with GSM 900 and 1800 handsets (used in Europe). Quad-band US phones will work, but to avoid global-roaming charges you'll need an unlocked handset that takes prepaid SIM cards from Australian providers such as **Telstra** (www.telstra.com), **Optus** (www.optus.com.au), **Virgin** (www.virginmobile.com.au) or **Vodafone** (www.vodafone.com.au).

TIPPING

Like the rest of Australia, tipping in Sydney isn't mandatory, but it's polite to tip hotel porters $2 per bag, and taxis and restaurant waiters around 10% of the charge.

TOURIST INFORMATION

There are City Host Information Kiosks at Circular Quay (Map p49, D4), Town Hall (Map p33, A5) and Martin Place (Map p33, B3), while **Tourism Australia** (www.australia.com) conducts customer relations through its efficient website. Also worth a try:

National Parks & Wildlife Service (NPWS; Map p49, D3; ☎ 9247 5033; www.npws .nsw.gov.au; Cadman's Cottage, 110 George St, The Rocks; ☼ 9.30am-4.30pm Mon-Fri, 10am-4.30pm Sat & Sun; 🚻 🚌 🛥 Circular Quay) Info on Sydney Harbour, Royal, Ku-ring-gai Chase and Blue Mountains national parks.

National Roads & Motorists Association (NRMA; Map p33, A3; ☎ 13 21 32, emergency assistance 13 11 11; 74-76 King St; ☼ 9am-5pm Mon-Fri; 🚻 Martin Place Ⓜ City Centre 🚌 George St buses) Provides 24-hour emergency roadside assistance and travel, insurance and accommodation advice.

Sydney Visitor Centre (www.sydneyvisit orcentre.com) Circular Quay (Map p49, C3; ☎ 9240 8788; cnr Argyle & Playfair Sts, The Rocks; ☼ 9.30am-5.30pm; 🚻 🚌 🛥 Circular Quay) Darling Harbour (Map pp66-7, C4; ☎ 9240 8788; ☼ 9.30am-5.30pm; 🚻 Town Hall Ⓜ Garden Plaza 🚌 Convention 🛥 Darling Harbour) Super comprehensive, also acting as an accommodation agency (last minute and in advance).

Tourism NSW (☎ 13 20 77; www.visitnsw .com.au) Airport (☎ 9667 6050; ☼ 5am-11pm) Statewide accommodation and travel advice.

Tourist Information Service (☎ 9669 5111; ☼ 7am-10pm) Sydney-centric information and accommodation phone service.

Travellers' Information Service (Map pp66-7, E7; ☎ 9281 9366; Sydney Coach Terminal, Eddy Ave; ☼ 6am-10.30pm; 🚻 🚕 Central Ⓜ Haymarket 🚌 George St buses) Helpful, busy office handling last-minute accommodation bookings, coach tickets, public transport information and maps.

TRAVELLERS WITH DISABILITIES

Most of Sydney's attractions are accessible to travellers with wheelchairs. All new or renovated venues cater for wheelchairs but older buildings are harder to access. Most of the National Trust's historic houses are at least partially accessible – abashed attendants can usually show you photos of inaccessible areas.

Taxis can usually accommodate wheelchairs; Sydney has a proliferation of parking spaces reserved for disabled drivers. Most of Sydney's major attractions offer hearing loops and sign language interpreters for hearing-impaired travellers. Check in advance.

For more info contact the following organisations:

City of Sydney (☎ 9265 9333; www.city ofsydney.nsw.gov.au) Lists venues with good wheelchair access.

Deaf Society of NSW (☎ 9893 8555; www .deafsocietynsw.org.au) Services, events and resources around Sydney.

Roads & Traffic Authority (☎ 13 22 13; www.rta.nsw.gov.au) For disabled parking permits.

Spinal Cord Injuries Australia (☎ 9661 8855; www.spinalcordinjuries.com.au) Publishes *Access Sydney*.

Vision Australia (☎ 1300 847 466; www .visionaustralia.org.au) Services, events and resources.

>INDEX

See also separate subindexes for See (p188), Shop (p189), Eat (p190), Drink (p191) and Play (p191).

000 map pages

000 map pages

000 map pages

INDEX

V

000 map pages